SHOW STOPPERS!
70 Easy-to-Present Classroom Art Lessons for Elementary Kids

SHOW STOPPERS!
70 Easy-to-Present Classroom Art Lessons for Elementary Kids
Gene Baer

PARKER PUBLISHING COMPANY
West Nyack, New York 10995

©1989 *by*
PARKER PUBLISHING COMPANY, INC.
West Nyack, NY

All rights reserved. No part of this book may be
reproduced in any form or by any means, without permission
in writing from the publisher.

10　9　8　7　6　5　4　3　2　1

Library of Congress Cataloging-in-Publication Data

Baer, Gene, 1927-
　Show stoppers! : 70 easy-to-present classroom art lessons for elementary kids / by Gene Baer.
　　p.　cm.
　　ISBN 0-13-809237-0
　1. Art—Study and teaching (Elementary)—United States.
I. Title.
N362.B34　1989
372.5'044—dc19　　　　　　　　　　　　　　　　89-2969
　　　　　　　　　　　　　　　　　　　　　　　　CIP

0-13-809237-0

PARKER PUBLISHING COMPANY
BUSINESS & PROFESSIONAL DIVISION
A division of Simon & Schuster
West Nyack, New York 10995

Printed in the United States of America

A Word from the Author

Between the covers of this book you will find ravenous bats that snap their jaws and flap their wings, nervous fish that hurl themselves high into the air, toothless trolls with chomping lips, wiggling mice that beg for food, shadowy monsters that flex their muscles and sniff the air, heads that talk, figures that dance, and whole cities that rise mysteriously from pristine planes of white paper.

You'll find jumping frogs, barking dogs, turkey hats, water bombs, and pictures that will delight in strange and unexpected ways . . .

The fourth in my ongoing series for Parker Publishing, *SHOW STOPPERS! 70 Easy-to-Present Classroom Art Lessons for Elementary Kids*, assumes no special art training on the part of the teacher. The instructions are precise, the language is clear, the procedural drawings are carefully keyed to the text, and—if you feel in need of further convincing—consider this: only a small handful of the lessons found in this book call for much more than paper, paste, pencils, scissors and crayons!

Furthermore I have a *very* strong hunch that *SHOW STOPPERS!* is destined to become the most popular book in this entire series. Why? Because it is packed with the kinds of explosive ideas that will make your kids stand up and cheer!

And for *whom* will they be cheering?

They will be cheering for YOU!

PAPER, PASTE, PENCILS, SCISSORS AND CRAYONS?

Like you, I too teach in an elementary school, and so the instructional materials available to me are probably much the same as those that can be found in your own classroom, or borrowed from the teacher next door! The only conceivable difference between my supplies and your supplies might be in the quality of schoolroom paste.

A lower grade of paste may *look* like paste and it may even be *creamier* than the real thing, but unless it does what it is supposed to do—and does it well—it is a shoddy form of piracy that does not deserve to be called paste at all!

Then what about glue; isn't a standard white glue a better adhesive than paste? True, but glue comes with a variety of other problems which include caps that need constant servicing and a dripping need for a lot of hawk-eyed supervision.

So—what's a poor teacher to do? My advice is to go with a good brand of paste (Crayola®, etc.). My second choice: white glue. And then, and only after all other possible alternatives have been explored, I suppose that we will just have to go with a cheap grade of paste—or go without!

PAPER, SIZE, ETC.

At first glance, it may seem that I have filled this book with a lot of unusual paper sizes (6" × 9", 4-1/2" × 6", etc.), but I assure you that I have done my best to see that all fractional sizes are governed—not by art or by whim—but by the necessary frugality that comes with the knowledge that neither one of us has unlimited access to art supplies!

STAPLING INSTRUCTIONS

Since most teachers feel themselves fortunate if they teach in a room that has *one* or, at most, *two* functioning classroom staplers, all stapling instructions have been written with this limitation in mind. If, however, you teach in a school that can supply individual staplers for everyone, by all means take advantage of your riches and encourage your kids to "staple it themselves"!

AND FINALLY . . .

I have written this book for all to enjoy, teachers and students alike; so, above all, relax . . . and have fun!

About the Author

Gene Baer is the K-8 art specialist for the Town of Tisbury on Martha's Vineyard, Massachusetts. He started teaching art after a successful career in illustration, beginning as an artist in the U.S. Army and a technical illustrator for industry. He has done extensive freelance commercial art and has sold cartoons to many national publications. Mr. Baer has also authored three other art instruction resources for K-8 teachers: *Paste, Pencils, Scissors and Crayons* (1979), *Imaginative Art Lessons for Kids and Their Teachers* (1982), and *Gene Baer's Wild & Wonderful Art Lessons* (1983). Recently, he sold his first children's book to Harper & Row. Entitled *Thump, Thump, Rat-a-Tat-Tat*, the book will be published in 1989.

To
Kara, Lissy, and Christian

Contents

A WORD FROM THE AUTHOR / v

1—SETTING THE STAGE / 1

*Art activities for the very young, the artisticly timid—
or for anyone else who cares to participate!*

Lesson 1
Mr. Eater Comes to Our Room / 1

Lesson 2
Submarine Sandwich Time! / 3

Lesson 3
Cutting Magic Shapes / 6

Lesson 4
Fishing for Fun / 10

Lesson 5
Worm in the Garden / 12

Lesson 6
Peek-A-Boo Buildings and House / 14

Lesson 7
Indian Village / 17

Lesson 8
Down to the Bottom of the. . . / 18

Lesson 9
A Visiting Rabbit / 20

Lesson 10
Familiar Faces / 22

Lesson 11
Puppies in a Box / 23

2—CURTAIN RAISERS / 27

Single session art projects

Lesson 1
Blabbermouth Puppets / 27

Lesson 2
Open for Business / 29

Lesson 3
Getting into Deep Water / 30

Lesson 4
Riding the Waves / 32

Lesson 5
Attack-Bats / 34

Lesson 6
Call of the Wild / 36

Lesson 7
Monster Rally / 39

Lesson 8
Bag People / 42

Lesson 9
Pop Architecture / 43

Lesson 10
Dinner Plate Turkeys / 47

Lesson 11
Turkey Hats / 48

Lesson 12
Turkeys and Turkey Pilgrims / 50

Lesson 13
There's No Place Like Home! / 52

Lesson 14
Raising a Pet Mouse / 55

Contents

Lesson 15
Santa with a Watermelon on His Head / 56

Lesson 16
Dashing Through the Snow / 59

Lesson 17
Super-Santa / 62

Lesson 18
Reindeer Land! / 63

Lesson 19
The World's Best Skating / 64

Lesson 20
Snow Hill / 66

Lesson 21
Dancin' for the Fun of It! / 69

Lesson 22
Traveling in the Fast Lane / 71

Lesson 23
Basket Filled with Love / 73

Lesson 24
Weaving with a Wobble / 74

Lesson 25
Seeing Through It All / 77

Lesson 26
World's Ugliest Trolls and Leprechauns / 79

Lesson 27
Salted Eggs / 82

Lesson 28
An Egg-Bearing Rabbit / 84

Lesson 29
How Does Your Garden Grow? / 86

Lesson 30
Flat-Bottomed Boat for All Occasions / 91

Lesson 31
Flap-Art / 93

Lesson 32
Paper Roses / 96

Lesson 33
Link-Weaving / 99

Lesson 34
Heads Up! / 101

Lesson 35
From Out of the Shadows... / 103

Lesson 36
Barkin' Dogs / 107

Lesson 37
Jumpin' Frogs / 110

Lesson 38
And Flyin' Fish / 113

3—MAGICAL IMPROVIZATIONS / 117

Instructional art activities that can be performed in only a few minutes or linked together with other improvizations to form lesson of nearly any length!

Lesson 1
Origami Cup / 117

Lesson 2
Flexasquare / 119

Lesson 3
A Couple of Real Bangers / 122

Lesson 4
Flying in the Wright Tradition / 125

Lesson 5
Score Keepers / 130

Lesson 6
Mr. Möbius and Mr. Baer / 131

Lesson 7
Squaring the Circle / 135

Lesson 8
Alive and Moving! / 137

Lesson 9
Nose Art / 140

Lesson 10
The Magic Hexagon / 141

Lesson 11
Drawing by Magic / 148

Lesson 12
Giving the Teacher a Hand! / 153

Lesson 13
Escape Artists / 166

Lesson 14
Origami Box and Water Bomb / 168

4—FULL-SCALE PRODUCTION NUMBERS / 173

This chapter contains many of my most cherished classroom secrets. While none of these lessons are short—and many require more than two or three classroom sessions to complete—ALL are easy to present, easy to do, and ALL lead to stunning conclusions.

Lesson 1
Black Magic / 173

Lesson 2
Pencil Pointillism / 176

Lesson 3
Full-Color Journalism / 177

Lesson 4
Washouts! / 182

Lesson 5
Sawing a Head in Half / 183

Lesson 6
Geodesic Creations / 185

Lesson 7
The Greatest Show Stopper of Them All! / 188

5—TRICKS, SHORTCUTS, AND ETCETERA... / 191

Box Making / 191

Circlecones / 192

Crayon Scrapers / 193

Eggs and Ovals / 193

Equilateral Triangles / 194

Measuring Strips, Straightedges, and Rulers / 195

Paper Straws / 197

Sailboating / 198

Scoring / 200

Staplers / 200

SHOW STOPPERS!
70 Easy-to-Present Classroom Art Lessons for Elementary Kids

1
Setting the Stage

Art Activities for the Very Young, the Artistically Timid—or for Anyone Else Who Cares to Participate!

If you were to be suddenly wrenched from your home, separated from your friends, herded into a holding room, and then lectured to by a cadre of complete strangers, would you call this experience frightening? Terrifying? Harrowing?

Of course you would. Ask any kid and they'll tell you the same thing: going to school is *not* easy!

That's why so many seasoned teachers like to begin the year with warm-up lessons, for they know, as you know, that what takes place in their classrooms during these first trauma-filled weeks is only setting the stage for the more demanding learning experiences which lie ahead.

And since all teachers, beginners and veterans alike can always use a fresh warm-up lesson, I would like to begin this book by sharing a few of my best.

Lesson 1
Mr. Eater Comes to Our Room

The kids are as nervous as a school of sardines at canning time: what they need now is the reassuring touch of a master teacher.

That's where *you* and Mr. Eater come in!

EACH CHILD WILL NEED:

- drawing paper
- paper plate
- scissors and crayons

TO PRESENT:

1. Begin by inviting your kids to use their crayons and drawing paper to "make things for Mr. Eater to eat."

Your introductory patter might go something like this: "Does Mr. Eater like pizza? Yes, Mr. Eater likes pizza. Let's see now, what else does Mr. Eater like: he likes apples...and cookies...and, well, he likes a lot of different kinds of foods. And he is coming to this room *soon*, so you had better get to work making things for Mr. Eater to eat!

As your kids get down to work coloring and cutting out the food for Mr. Eater's visit, your job is to walk over to the classroom door, peek out into the hall, and then return to make your report. "I just looked out," you say to your kids, "and although he is not yet in sight, I can hear him coming; so you had better get to work because I *know* he's going to be hungry!

"Does Mr. Eater like oranges?" you ask aloud as you begin to wander about the room to inspect the table preparations. "Oh, yes, Mr. Eater likes oranges. Does he like to eat *books*? Oh, yes, Mr. Eater *loves* books." And as you continue to lengthen the list of Mr. Eater's favorite foods, be sure to add in more than a fair share of other indigestible suggestions. ("Does Mr. Eater like to eat *cars*? Oh, yes, Mr. Eater *loves* to eat cars...")

As the mood of the classroom continues to mellow, your hallway reports should become increasingly preposterous. ("Oh, yes, I can see him now. He's eating the wall just outside the principal's office!" or "Whoops—he must be famished. He just ate the water fountain!")

By the time Mr. Eater has gobbled up half the hallway, the time is right to give each child a paper plate and to move into the final part of this lesson.

2. Using a paper plate of your own as a demonstration piece, turn the plate upside down, draw a pair of large eyes and a simple nose on the lower half of the plate, and have your kids do the same. The remainder of the "face" is then crayoned in as suggested here.

3. And that's that! Once the plates are folded in half, *presto*! Mr. Eater has arrived—and just in time for lunch!

Setting the Stage

4. Using your own work-along Mr. Eater as a gobbling hand puppet, you begin to circulate around the room so that *your* Mr. Eater can sample the various treats that have been prepared for his visit.

5. And when cleanup time finally arrives, the kids should be the first to know that Mr. Eater does *not* like scraps. He picks them up in his mouth and he *spits* them into the trash!

Lesson 2
Submarine Sandwich Time!

What do the kids in your class call a sandwich made from a long loaf of Italian bread sliced down the middle and loaded with cold cuts, cheese, lettuce, tomatoes, onions, etc.? A *hero*, a *sub*, a *poor boy*, a *grinder*...?

Call it what you will, but if your class is hungry for a *fun* lesson, this is it!

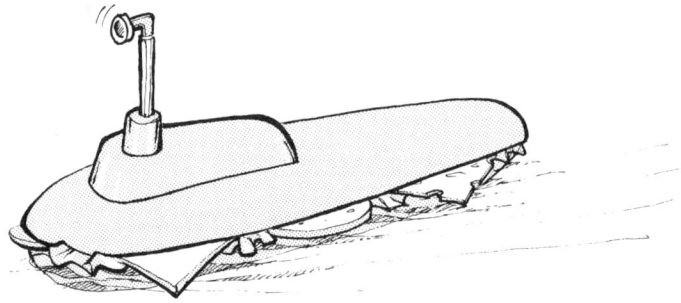

EACH CHILD WILL NEED:

- 7" × 12" manila drawing paper
- 4-1/2" × 6" construction paper in the following colors: meat brown, cheese yellow, lettuce green, tomato red and onion white. (Other ingredients optional!)
- a shared 3-1/2" (watercup size) circle pattern
- 1/2 page newspaper
- pencil, scissors and paste

THE TEACHER WILL NEED:

a stapler

TO PRESENT:

1. To make the basic sandwich, have your kids fold their 7" × 12" manila paper lengthwise and round or clip* the corners as suggested here.

2. The "meat" is then cut into strips and, with the help of a little "Italian mayonnaise" (paste), secured to the open face of the sandwich in the manner shown here. (It is important to note that a generous portion of the "meat" is purposely arranged so that it extends well beyond the side of the sandwich.)

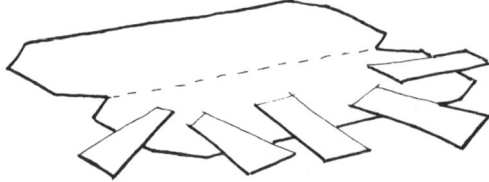

---

* Many young children find the task of cutting a rounded corner to be an impossible task. If this problem should arise—or if you anticipate such a problem—be sure to recommend the use of the clipped corner ("as can often be found on some of the best brands of Italian bread").

3. The "cheese" is then prepared and secured in the same way. The "lettuce", however, to be more lettuce-like, should be torn—not cut—before securing to the face of the sandwich in the same manner as the meat and the cheese.

And once they have come this far, I am sure that your kids can figure out what to do with their "tomato" paper.

4. But if your kids think that they have had fun up to this point, they haven't seen anything yet, for it is in the making of the "onion rings" that we now come upon the *piece de rèsistance!*

To make the onion rings, have your kids trace their circle patterns onto the white paper. These traced circles are then cut out, folded in half, and cut "rainbow-style" as indicated by the dotted lines. And when the resulting snippets open up into full size *onion rings*—your kids will be absolutely delighted with this discovery!

5. Then, once the onion ring excitement begins to die down, have your kids line up at the desk to have *one* end and the open side of the sandwich stapled together. The "Italian stuffing" (the newspaper) is then wrinkled up and shoved in from the open end to give the sandwich its convincing bread-like bulk.

The stuffed sandwich is then stapled at the open end and set aside *for a late afternoon snack*!

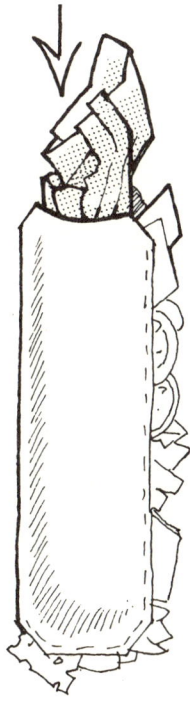

Setting the Stage

Lesson 3
Cutting Magic Shapes

Create a sense of wonder in a child and you have opened a door that can lead to profound discoveries. *Cutting Magic Shapes* accomplishes this impossible-sounding miracle using little more than paper, scissors, and a shared sense of accomplishment.

EACH CHILD WILL NEED:

- construction paper in the following sizes:
    - 4 1/2" × 6"
    - 6" × 9"
    - 3" × 18"
    - 9" squares*
- scissors

Activity 1: "Cut Out a Piece — Skip a Piece"

TO PRESENT:

1. Begin by showing your kids the difference between "cutting lines" and "cutting out pieces."

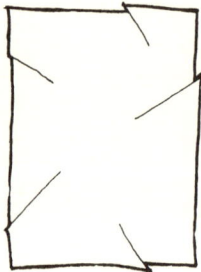 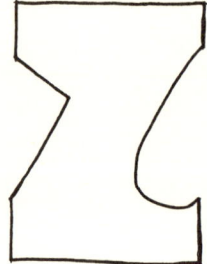

---

* If these dimensions puzzle you, see page vi for comments under *Paper, Size, Etc.*.

Setting the Stage

Then pass out sheets of 4-1/2" × 6" construction paper and invite your kids to "cut out a piece—skip a piece" as suggested here.

2. Once this basic skill has been mastered, have your kids repeat this same exercise using a *folded* sheet of 4-1/2" × 6" paper, open and enjoy!

3. Now have your kids repeat this same exercise using a sheet of 6" × 9" construction paper folded into quadrants.

4. And for the last exercise in this introductory paper cutting activity, have your kids "do it again" using the 3" × 18" strip of construction paper folded into lengthwise quarters.

 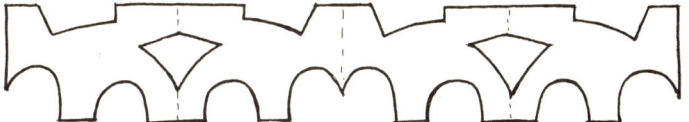

Activity 2: Stretching Paper

TO PRESENT:

1. Holding high a sheet of 6" × 9" construction paper, you boldly state that you intend to cut off a strip that will exceed the height of the tallest child in your class!

Since none of your kids will take this proposal seriously, you will be instantly rewarded with the kind of amused attention that is normally reserved for predictable disasters. But taking advantage of your position at center stage, you wait until the last derisive comment has rippled through the classroom before you hold up your scissors and dramatically begin to perform your "miracle" by cutting the paper as suggested here. (The closer the cuts, the further the paper will stretch.)

2. And once the show is over, your job is to pass out the rest of the 6" × 9" construction paper and let your young magicians "do it themselves"!

Activity 3: "Help Me—I'm Lost!"

TO PRESENT:

Now that you have irrevocably captured the imagination of your audience, your next "trick" can be performed with the complete assurance that the stage is now incontestably yours!

1. As you hold high a 9" square of construction paper, you reassure your audience that if they thought that the last trick was a good one, "this one will be even *better!*"

Then, using as much showmanship as you can muster, you begin to cut into your paper along the squaraling* route indicated.

---

* A *squaral* (in case you forget to ask) is a spiral with square corners.

Setting the Stage 9

And take your time! Cut for a while, display, cut for a while, etc. And as you do this, tell the story of a Mr. Scissors who finds himself imprisoned within the ever-shrinking walls of the surrounding paper. (Hence the title: *Help Me—I'm Lost!*)

As the story continues, raise you hands higher, cut some more, and then stop again for all to marvel at Mr. Scissors' dilemma. From here on out, continue this stop-and-go routine until you are finally standing triumphantly on a chair with your paper strip dangling all the way to the floor as shown.

2. *Now* comes the climax to the whole performance. Inviting a nearby child to pick up the dangling end of your magic strip, you then slowly back off to s-t-r-e-t-c-h the paper to its fragile limits. Done properly, this paper strip should be long enough to nearly reach across the room!

And now that you have had *your* fun, let your kids have theirs. Pass out the 9″ construction paper squares and watch what happens!

Lesson 4
Fishing for Fun

Like *Mr. Eater Comes to Our Room* (page 1), this lesson begins with a paper plate, but, unlike Mr. Eater, *Fishing for Fun* comes baited with a "real" hook. Catch it if you can!

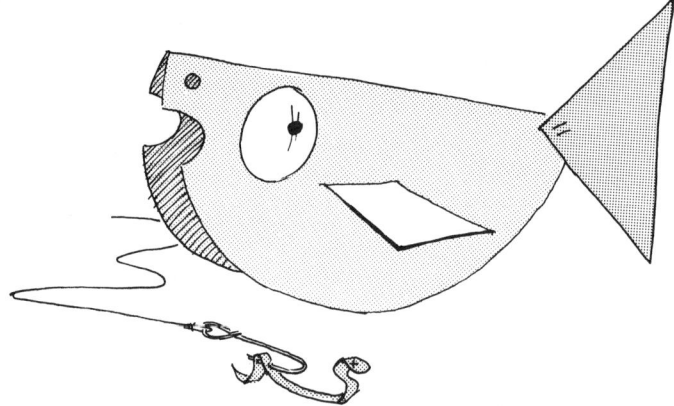

EACH CHILD WILL NEED:

- a paper plate
- tagboard (or other pattern-weight paperboard):
    diagonal half of a 4-1/2" square
    2" × 6" strip
- one or more red "worm" papers
- crayons
- a piece of string with an attached "hook" (see the preparations to follow.)

THE TEACHER WILL NEED:

- a stapler
- a hand-held paper punch
- a single-edge razor blade or hobby knife, and a desk-protecting sheet of cardboard

PREPARATIONS:

Tackle-making Instructions: To participate in this fishing expedition, your kids will need barbless hooks and short lengths of string. Here's how:

To Make a Classroom Tackle Knot: If you already know how to make an overhand knot, you have all the skills necessary to set up an efficient one-person, tackle-making assembly line.

To Make a Classroom Fishing Hook: Using a paperclip, simply follow the wordless instructions shown here.

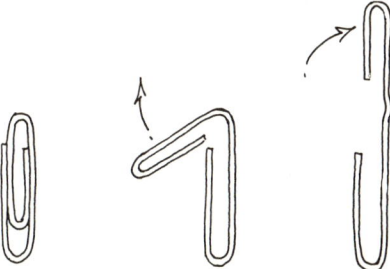

To Assemble: Now that everything is ready to go, the rest is easy: just thread the loop of the string over the open end of the eye of the hook and bend to secure as shown here.

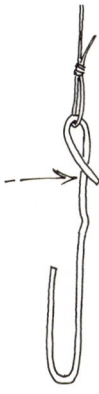

TO PRESENT:

1. Have your kids draw two large eyes at the bottom of their paper plates as suggested here. Then invite them to use their crayons "to color everything *except* the whites of their eyes."

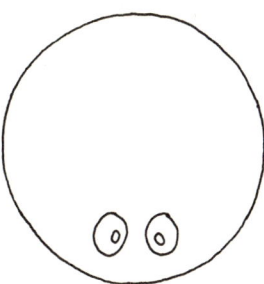

2. The triangular piece of paperboard is to become the tail; the 2" × 6", the pectoral fin. And both, of course, will be in need of careful coloring! And while your kids

are busy doing all of this, it is your job to fold their completed plates in half so that you can use your razor blade to cut pectoral slits of an appropriate length.

3. All that's needed now to bring this fish to life is a punched "nose" a stapled tail, and an assembled fin, as shown. (See illustration at the top of page 10.)

Then—pass out the fishing tackle and watch what happens!

Lesson 5
Worm in the Garden

I really don't know what invited this wiggly worm into my creative subconscious, but—unlike the Serpent that spoiled the picnic in the Garden of Eden—this little creature will bring nothing but happiness!

EACH CHILD WILL NEED:

- practice paper
- 12" × 18" drawing paper
- construction paper:
    6" × 18" green
    2-1/4" × 12" red
- paste, pencils, scissors and crayons

THE TEACHER WILL NEED:

- a stapler

Setting the Stage

TO PRESENT:

1. Begin by using the practice paper to introduce your kids to some elementary flower-drawing concepts, as suggested here.

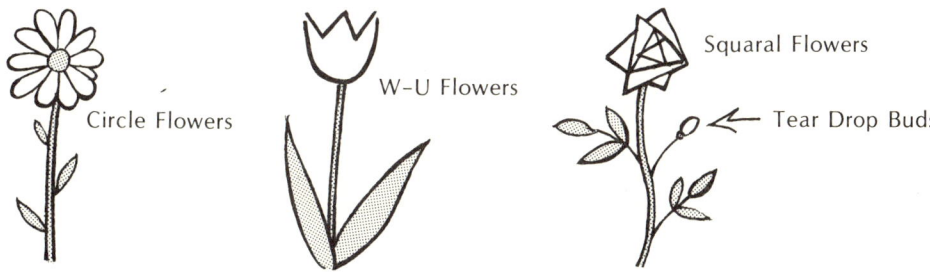

2. Once the practice session has run its course, have your kids fold their 6" × 18" green papers in half lengthwise, unfold, and then "cut the grass," stopping short of the fold as shown here.

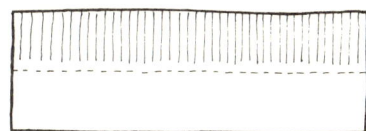

The green paper is then refolded, fitted over the bottom of the drawing paper, and then stapled at the corners as shown.

3. Once the grass is in place, invite your kids to draw in the flowers—being sure that "the stems go behind the grass and all the way down to the 'ground'!"

4. The 2-1/4" × 12" red paper is then folded "crooked," as suggested, and brought to life by transforming one end into a head, pointing the other into a tail, and by securing each fold with a staple as shown here.

 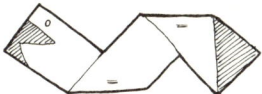

5. And the rest of the lesson is all playtime, for as soon as your kids finish their worms, the grass-high game of low-level hide and seek begins!

Lesson 6
Peek-A-Boo Buildings and Houses

Invented by the same collective mind that brought you the advent calendar, *Peek-A-Boo Buildings and Houses* are always in season!

First Version: Peek-A-Boo Buildings and Houses for the Very Young

EACH CHILD WILL NEED:

- 12" × 18" drawing or construction paper
- pencil, scissors and crayons

THE TEACHER WILL NEED:

- a sheet of 9" × 12" cardboard and a single-edge razor blade or hobby knife

TO PRESENT:

1. Using the 12" × 18" drawing or construction paper and the instructions given below, have your kids begin by making either a building or a house.

To Make the Basic Building: Simply fold the paper in half widthwise.

To Make the Basic House: The paper is folded in half widthwise, a centrally-placed dot is penciled onto one of the short edges, and slanting lines are drawn as shown here. Have your kids cut on these lines through "both pieces" of the folded paper.

Setting the Stage

2. As your kids finish up this preliminary work, have them line up by your desk to have their front windows and doors cut out as suggested here. (*That*, of course, is what the razor blade and the cardboard are for!)

The buildings and/or houses are then returned to their owners for both exterior and interior improvements as suggested here.

Second Version: Peek-A-Boo Buildings and Houses for Slightly Older Kids

Although we live in a near-shutterlesss society, shutters *always* evoke a visceral response in kids!

EACH CHILD WILL NEED:
- two sheets of 12" × 18" drawing paper
- pencils and crayons

THE TEACHER WILL NEED:
- a stapler
- a single-edge razor blade or hobby knife, and a sheet of 12" × 18" cardboard

TO PRESENT:

1. Invite your kids to draw a street scene but to leave all windows blank.
2. Your job, then, is to wait until this lesson is well underway before you staple each partially completed street scene to a second sheet of drawing paper, as suggested here.

3. When all the drawings have been stapled to their second sheets, your next assignment is to slide your cardboard between the stapled sheets and to use your razor blade to open all doors, windows and shutters.

But Please Note: While most kids will probably prefer traditional shutters (see the illustration on the left), be prepared for requests to have windows "open the other way," as shown here on the right.

4. In any case, once the windows and doors are opened—*your* job is done. The kids will do the rest!

Version Three: Two-View Peek-A-Boo Buildings and Houses

As a variation on the preceding lesson, teach your kids how to draw their houses and buildings in "two-view," as shown.

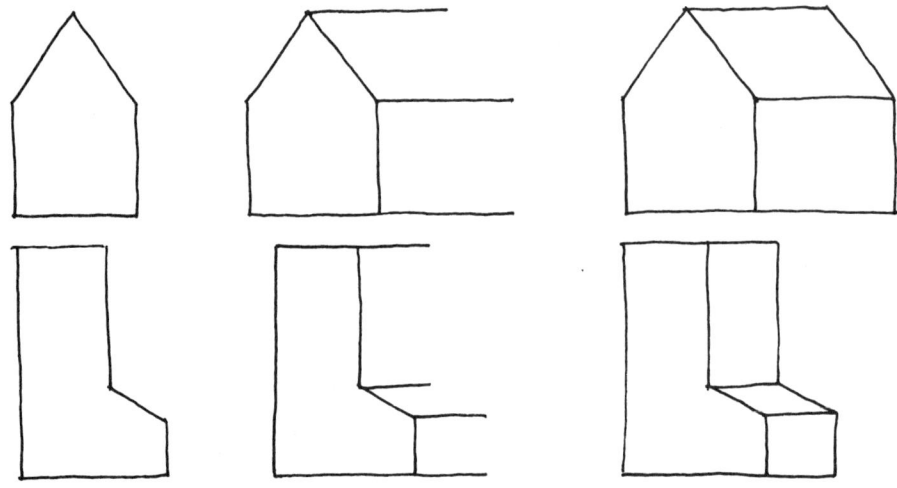

Setting the Stage

Lesson 7
Indian Village

There are many ways to celebrate our pre-Columbian heritage, but few are as simple to present as this child-size Indian campsite!

EACH CHILD WILL NEED:

- one-half of a paper plate
- drawing paper:
    - 12" × 18"
    - 2" × 6"
    - 3" × 3/4"
    - 3" × 3/8"
- construction paper:
    - scraps of fire red and log brown
- paste, scissors and crayons

THE TEACHER WILL NEED:

- a stapler

TO PRESENT:

1. Have your kids color their paper plates "rainbow-style." The completed rainbows are then quickly transformed into colorful tipis and stapled in place as shown here.

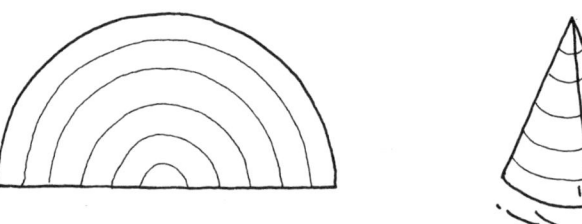

2. The 2" × 6" drawing paper is colored "canoe color" and stapled as shown.

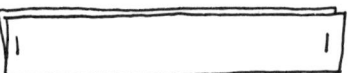

3. The Indians are made from 3" lengths of drawing paper as suggested here. (While older children can assemble their own, younger kids may do better with pre-stapled units.)

4. The greater part of the 12" × 18" paper is reserved for the land on which the tipi will sit, the remaining part can then be colored blue and used for launching canoes, catching fish, etc. And the red and brown papers will supply all the material necessary to build a substantial, Indian-style bonfire!

Enjoy!

Lesson 8
Down to the Bottom of the...

Wherever fish can swim, the imagination is free to roam. Here is an art lesson that does just that!

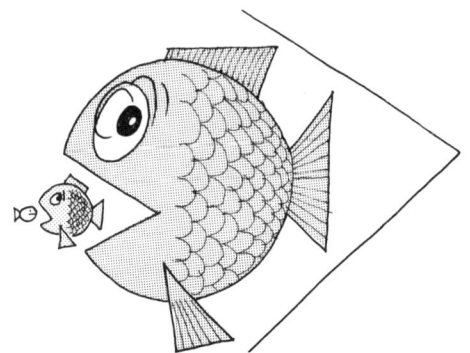

Setting the Stage

EACH CHILD WILL NEED:

- construction paper:
    - 12" × 18" blue "water"
    - 4-1/2" × 6" assorted "fish" colors
    - 2-1/4" squares of assorted "fish tail" colors
    - 3" × 9" green "seaweed" paper
- manila drawing paper: 4-1/2" × 6" (two each)
- shared 3-1/2" (watercup size) circle pattern
- paste, pencil, scissors and crayons

TO PRESENT:

1. Have your kids trace the circle patterns onto the 4-1/2" × 6" fish papers. Once traced, these circles are cut out and brought to life with the help of a snipped-out mouth, a crayoned eye, and a tail made from one of the diagonal halves of the 4-1/2" square. For more sophisticated fish, have your kids use the remainder of their tail papers to add additional fins.

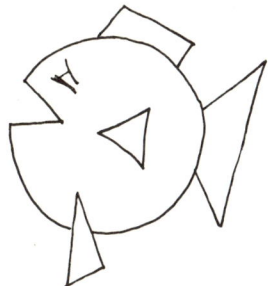

2. These fish are then pasted to the blue "water" paper, and strips of green seaweed are added to make the fish feel at home.

3. From here on, the possibilities are endless, but I think that you'll find the following suggestions just too good to ignore!

Clams: Clams are made by folding the 4-1/2" × 6" manila paper widthwise and tracing the circle pattern as shown here. When your kids cut on this line through the double thickness of the folded paper—*presto*! It's chowder time!

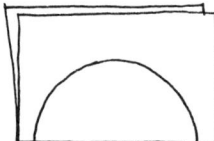

Sunken Treasure: Have your kids fold their 4-1/2" × 6" manila paper lengthwise as shown here. Add a (broken) lock and fill with doubloons and jewels!

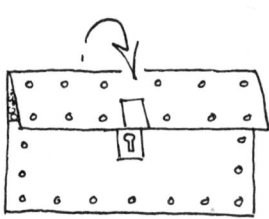
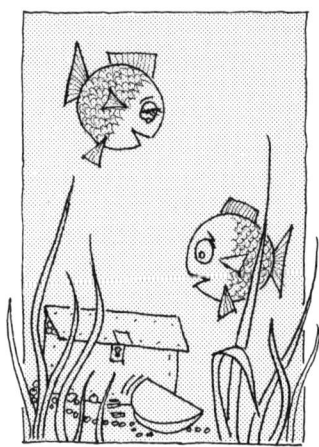

Lesson 9
A Visiting Rabbit

Easter lessons are a dime a dozen, but a rabbit *this* personable comes by but once in a lifetime!

Setting the Stage

EACH CHILD WILL NEED:
- a lunch bag
- a "cotton ball" (or the modern, non-cotton equivalent known as a *cosmetic puff*)
- construction paper:
    - 4-1/2" × 6" and 6" × 9" brown
    - 3" × 4-1/2" white
    - 3" × 9" orange
    - 3" × 9" green
- paste, pencils, scissors and crayons

TO PRESENT:

1. Begin by inviting your kids to use their orange and green paper to assemble a carrot.

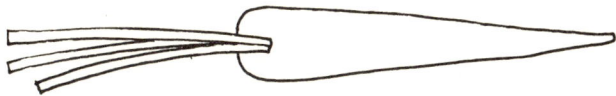

2. A large paper-filling oval is then drawn on the 4-1/2" × 6" brown paper and cut out. The white paper is for making eyes and teeth, and the nose and the cheeks can be drawn in crayon, as shown.

3. The 6" × 9" brown paper is cut into two lengthwise sections and trimmed into ears, and then everything is assembled and pasted into place.

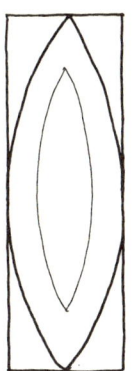

4. And the "cotton ball" goes right where you think it should go! "So, what's up, Doc?"

Lesson 10
Familiar Faces

Mother, father, brother, sister . . . in this lesson, the child never really leaves home!

EACH CHILD WILL NEED:

- drawing paper:
    3", 6", and 9" squares
    1" × 6", 1-1/2" × 9". and 1/2" × 3" strips
- paste, scissors and crayons

THE TEACHER MAY NEED:

- a small stapler, or, preferably, *stapling pliers**

TO PRESENT:

1. Have your kids roll up the 6" square into a tube and paste or staple.
"This is *you*!" You explain to your kids, as you demonstrate how a flattened tube can be made to resemble a person.

---

* For a discussion on staplers see "Tricks, Shortcuts, Etcetera . . .", page 200.

Setting the Stage

2. Once the front and back of this first figure is completed in crayon, have your kids cut about halfway down each fold to accommodate the 1" × 6" arm paper. The top of the figure is then sealed with paste (or stapled), the bottom is squeezed to restore the basic cylindrical shape, and the finished figure is encouraged to "find its feet."

3. Once the first figure has been completed, the whole family can be brought to life in the same way. The 9" squares pair with the 1-1/2" × 9" arms to make the adult members of the family, and the 3" squares and the 1/2" × 3" strips are all that is needed to make the younger brothers and sisters!

AND FINALLY:

Here is a child-size suggestion that was given to me by one of my favorite kindergarten classes: to make "hugging arms," simply join the hands with a dab of paste!

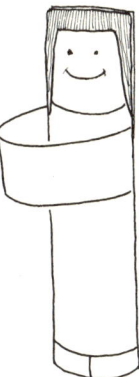

Lesson 11
Puppies in a Box

If there are two things that kids love, it's art lessons with moving parts and—*puppies*!

EACH CHILD WILL NEED:
- 9" × 12" assorted "box" colors

- matching sets of assorted "puppy" colors:
    4-1/2" square
    4-1/2" × 6"
- 4-1/2" × 10" (or any other convenient size) sheets of newspapers to line the puppy boxes
- 6" × 9" manila drawing paper
- paste, pencils, scissors and crayons

THE TEACHER WILL NEED:

- a stapler

TO PRESENT:

1. Have your kids fold their 9" × 12" papers in half lengthwise, to be set aside for later.

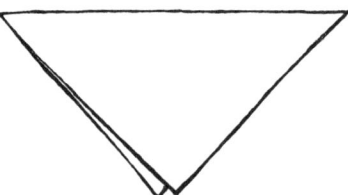

2. The 4-1/2" square is then folded in half diagonally to make the basic puppy head, and the corners adjoining this fold are bent over to make the ears.

3. Now, while your kids are busy adding details (crayoning the gums, adding teeth, coloring the ears, etc.), *your* job is to travel the room to staple the free corners of the folded 9" × 12" papers to complete the basic "puppy box." (See illustration at the top of the next page.)

Setting the Stage

4. While the creatively gifted will have no trouble turning the 4-1/2" × 6" sheet of paper into a puppy's body, here is an easy-to-learn suggestion for those who may need help:

Simply invite your kids to think of this 4-1/2" × 6" paper as a "wall". Tell them to place a door "that isn't a door" in the center of this "wall". Then cut out. (In other words, "Remove the 'door' and keep the 'wall'!")

5. The two-piece puppies (plus tails made from the leftover "doors") are then assembled with paste or glue.

6. The newspapers are then folded lengthwise and used to line the boxes (in case of accidents!); and the 6" × 9" papers. Why, they can be used for dozens of important things. Perhaps the puppies would like something to eat? Maybe a bone? A bowl of dog food? Or maybe just a ball to play with?

Or, better still, just turn this whole problem over to your kids. *They'll* know what to do!

2
Curtain Raisers

Single Session Art Projects

Lesson 1
Blabbermouth Puppets

These paper cup puppets are the best of their kind that I have ever seen. Why? Because not only are these creatures easy to make, but their non-stop mouths are as wide as their heads are tall!

EACH CHILD WILL NEED:

- construction paper:
    9" × 12" assorted pastel "face" colors
    scraps of red "nose" and "eyeball" white
    3" × 4-1/2" assorted "hair" colors
- 6" × 9" drawing paper
- paste, pencil, scissors and crayons

TO PRESENT:

1. One step short of being a paper cup, the *Blabbermouth Puppet* begins with 9" × 12" pastel construction paper and the origami directions that begin on page 117. When your kids reach that point in the cup lesson where the results correspond to below, stop.

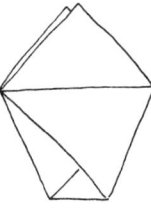

2. Now instead of turning down both top flaps as in the cup lesson, turn down only the front flap as shown, and paste.

3. Turn this folded paper around and position it as shown. Add a red construction paper nose, white construction paper eyeballs, and round the chin. The 3" × 9" pastel remainder from Step #1 will supply the ear paper, and the rest . . . well, by the time that you reach this stage in the lesson, further instructions will not be necessary!

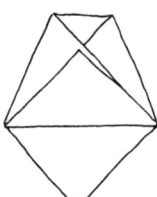 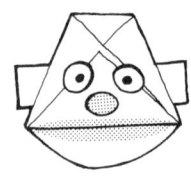

4. And the 6" × 9" drawing paper? That's for the body!

Curtain Raisers

Operating Instructions: To get the Blabbermouth to open its mouth—simply press in on both ends of the lips as shown on page 27!

Lesson 2
Open for Business

Sometimes the best classroom lessons are those that are so simple that even a child can understand them—try *Open for Business* and you'll see what I mean!

EACH CHILD WILL NEED:

- 12" × 18" drawing paper
- shared template made from a sheet of 6" × 18" tagboard or other pattern-weight paperboard. (See the following *Preparations*.)

THE TEACHER WILL NEED:

- single-edge razor blade or hobby knife
- 6" × 18" sheet of cardboard

PREPARATIONS:

Once you have positioned six dots onto a sheet of 6" × 18" tagboard (or other pattern-weight paperboard) as shown, use a sharp instrument (such as a compass point) to turn each of these dots into holes large enough to accommodate the point of a classroom pencil.

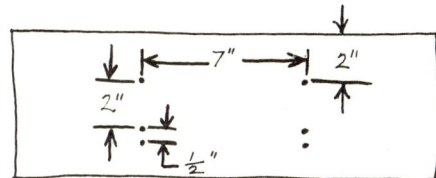

TO PRESENT:

1. Begin by explaining to your kids that today's problem features some kind of a stand: a refreshment stand, a circus, fair, or carnival stand, a roadside vegetable stand,

or maybe even a dockside bait stand. And while your kids are considering this idea, have them fold their papers in half lengthwise and use their paperboard patterns to position the six dots onto their drawing paper.

2. The dots, you explain, are going to be used to define the limits of the window area of the stand. At this point, have your kids use their pencils to connect the dots and to begin to draw the rest of their pictures. And then, in a voice usually reserved for "do it—or die!" instructions, you add, "But do *not* draw or color in any part of the window itself. Why? You'll see 'why' in just a few minutes!"

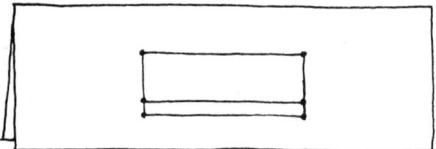 

3. Once the drawings are underway, invite your kids—one at a time—to line up at your desk. Then, once you have inserted a sheet of protective cardboard between the flaps of each drawing, use your razor blade or hobby knife to cut on the heavy lines. And once cut, fold out the window and counter flap.

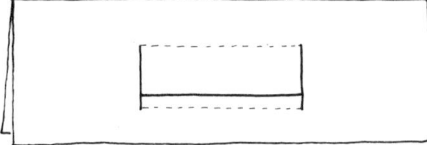 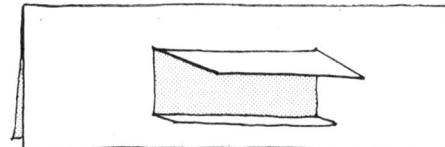

4. The moment that your kids see their windows open and their counter tops folded out and "opened for business", the rest is easy! The "board" window can either be left as is or transformed into an "awning." (See illustration at the top of page 29.) Either way, *Open for Business* is the kind of lesson that kids love.

You will too!

Lesson 3
Getting into Deep Water

Whether your kids are sailors or landlubbers, here is an inspired bit of paper folding that everyone will enjoy!

EACH CHILD WILL NEED:
- practice paper

Curtain Raisers

- 4-1/2" × 6" drawing paper
- construction paper:
    3" × 9" assorted "boat colors" with additional scraps of same
    12" × 18" light blue
- paste, pencil, scissors and crayons

TO PRESENT:

1. Have your kids fold their 3" × 9" boat papers in half lengthwise and *Sailboat** the ends as shown. Paste folded corner flaps to boat and set aside to dry.

2. Since a certain percentage of your kids will probably have difficulty drawing a figure in anything but a standing position, now would be as good a time as any to introduce your class to some of the concepts involved in drawing a seated figure. For one approach that always gets results:

- Draw a "fat" chair.
- Remove the back leg.
- Add a head and a foot.
- And the rest is easy!

3. Now—let's change the pace for a moment or two while we return to our work at the shipyards:

To Install Seats Amidship: These seats are easy to make. Simply fold a piece of construction paper and paste into place.

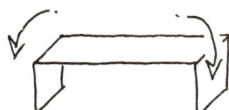 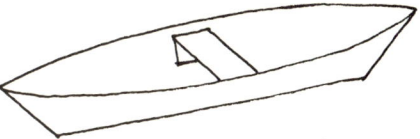

---

* See "Tricks, Shortcuts, Etcetera . . ." under *Sailboating* pages 198 and 199.

To Install Seats at Bow or Stern: Since these seats are triangular in shape, instruct your kids to draw a triangle of the proper size, add two side flaps, fold, and paste into position.

4. Once the boats have been made seaworthy, have your kids use their 4-1/2" × 6" drawing paper to draw a seated figure of appropriate size.

And once these figures have been crayoned in and cut out with scissors, invite your kids to paste both the *passenger* and the *midsection* (only) of the boat onto their 12" × 18" drawing paper.

5. And that's all that *you'll* have to do—your kids will take over from here!

Lesson 4
Riding the Waves

Used as a rowboat or outfitted with a motor, here is another versatile craft that my kids have used with great success to transport everyone from Pilgrims to pleasure seekers. Take it for a run or save it for Thanksgiving; either way, *Riding the Waves* will make for a memorable classroom outing!

EACH CHILD WILL NEED:

- construction paper:
    12" × 18" gray
    5" × 18" water blue
    6" × 12" boat paper
- 6" × 9" drawing paper
- pencil, scissors and crayons

Curtain Raisers

THE TEACHER WILL NEED:

- a stapler

TO PRESENT:

1. Have your kids fold their 5" × 18" blue construction paper in half lengthwise, unfold, and trim one of the long sides in a wavy fashion.

2. The 6" × 12" boat paper is then folded in half lengthwise and either stapled "as is" or with "improvements."

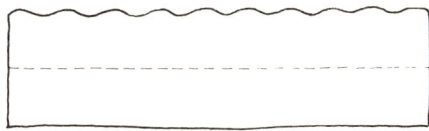

3. As you begin to staple each folded "water" paper to a sheet of 12" × 18" gray background paper as shown here, it is time to invite your kids to use their 6" × 9" drawing papers to "make the passengers"!

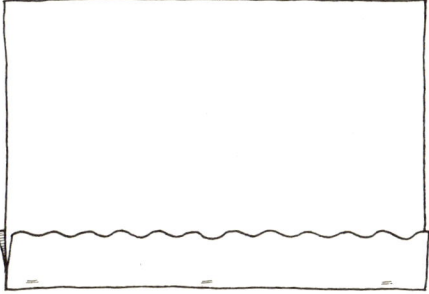

AND FINALLY:

Once your kids understand that their boats are designed to travel the waterways, *your* part of the lesson is over. The background will take care of itself!

Lesson 5
Attack-Bats

Every now and then I stumble upon a lesson that is so good that I feel like cheering. *This* is one of those lessons!

EACH CHILD WILL NEED:

- construction paper:
    - 9" square "head" paper
    - 6" × 18" "body" paper
    - 2-1/4" × 4-1/2" red "mouth" paper
    - scraps of white "eye" paper
    - strips of red "tongue" paper
- a shared pattern (see *Preparations*)
- paste, pencils, scissors and crayons

THE TEACHER WILL NEED:

- a stapler (preferably *stapling pliers**)

PREPARATIONS:

Using a sheet of 6" × 18" tagboard (or other pattern-weight paperboard) and the dimensions shown, it is your job to prepare enough patterns for sharing.

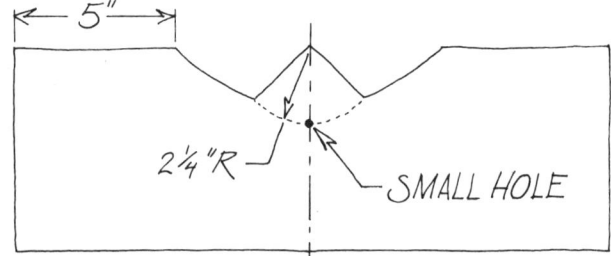

TO PRESENT:

1. Using the instructions found on pages 119–121, have your kids use their "head" paper to construct a *Flexasquare*.

2. Have your kids use the hole in the paperboard pattern to transfer a penciled dot to their 6" × 18" construction paper and to trace the lines that form the "shoulder" jogs. The traced jogs are then cut out, a line is cut from the apex of the "neck" to the penciled dot, and the rest of the body is sketched in.

3. While your kids are busy working on the bodies of their creatures, it's your job to staple each flexasquare so that only one of the alternate "mouths" will open.

---

* See "Tricks, Shortcuts, Etcetera . . ." under *Staplers* (page 200)

Once the stapling is complete, invite your kids to use their white paper to make eyes and to paste them into position.

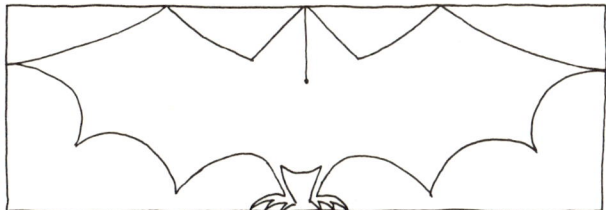

When cut in half widthwise, the 2-1/4" × 4-1/2" red paper will surrender two 2-1/4" squares which will, in turn, fit perfectly into the "mouth" to make the "gums." Tongue and teeth, of course, are optional!

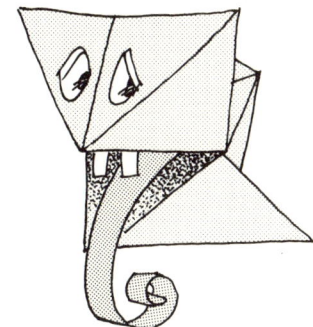

4. The rest is just a matter of stapling: insert the twin triangles of the "neck" into the rear pockets of the "chin" and staple.

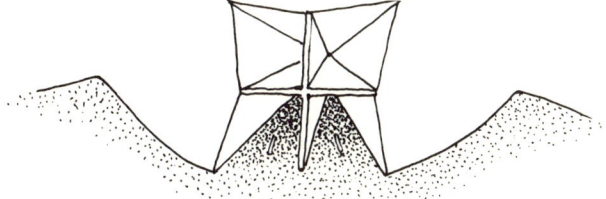

AND FINALLY:

Step back and admire!

And if you suggest to your kids that these creatures are always hungry for scraps, you'll be delighted to see dozens of ravenous scavengers winging their way across the room to surrender large mouthfuls of paper scraps into the classroom wastebasket!

Lesson 6
Call of the Wild

Wherever you are—they call for *you!*

Activity 1: Animal Masks for Little Kids

EACH CHILD WILL NEED:

- construction paper:
    12" square "animal" color*
    maybe a sheet of 4-1/2" × 6" white
- shared 11-1/2" circle pattern
- paste pencil, scissors and crayons

THE TEACHER WILL NEED:

- a stapler
- possibly a hand-held paper punch

---

* *Fur* colors or *fanciful* colors? One of us has to decide!

Curtain Raisers

TO PRESENT:

1. Have your kids trace the 11-1/2" circle pattern onto their 12" square of construction paper, add ears, and cut out.

2. Classroom masks can be designed to be worn or to be displayed. Those that have eye holes are more easily understood by children but are generally less decorative than the more colorful and imaginative eyes that can be designed from cut and pasted paper.

If you and your kids decide to take the more decorative route, no further eye-making instructions are necessary, but if eye holes are desired—the following instructions should prove to be helpful:

To Make Eye Holes:

After having your kids fold their masks in half, *your* job is to travel the room with your paper punch to punch starter holes. Those starter holes can then be enlarged with scissors to any size or shape that the child desires.

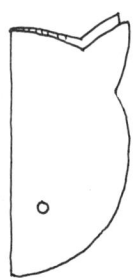

3. After the eyes have been completed, have your kids crayon on a nose and cut to the center of this nose on the heavy line.

4. And that's it! *Circlecone* and paste!*

Activity 2: Animal Masks for Older Kids

EACH CHILD WILL NEED:

- construction paper:
    12" square "animal color"** and a matching sheet of 4-1/2" × 6"
    4-1/2" × 6" pink
    4-1/2" × 6" red
    maybe a sheet of 4-1/2" × 6" white
- shared 3-1/2" (watercup size) circle pattern
- paste, pencil, scissors and crayons

THE TEACHER WILL NEED:

- a stapler
- possibly a hand-held paper punch

TO PRESENT:

1. Invite your kids to use their 12" square of construction paper to create a mouthless creature. Cut on the heavy line.

2. The eyes can then either be made from white paper or punched out as described in Step 2 of *Animal Masks for Little Kids* (see page 36).

---

* See "Tricks, Shortcuts, Etcetera . . ." under *Circlecones*. (Page 192.)

** See footnote on page 36.

Curtain Raisers

3. The pattern is used for tracing a circle on the pink paper. The pink circle is then cut out and a smaller circle of red is pasted in the center.

4. And the rest is easy—just *Circlecone** the mask and staple on the mouth as shown at the top of page 38.

Lesson 7
Monster Rally

Masks can be as flat as tax forms or as full-blown as balloons, but child-size instructions for a full 360° mask are not easy to find. Here, however, is one of the best!

EACH CHILD WILL NEED:

- colored construction paper:
    18" × 24" and assorted smaller sizes as needed
- shared patterns (See *Preparations* below)
- paste, pencil, scissors and crayons

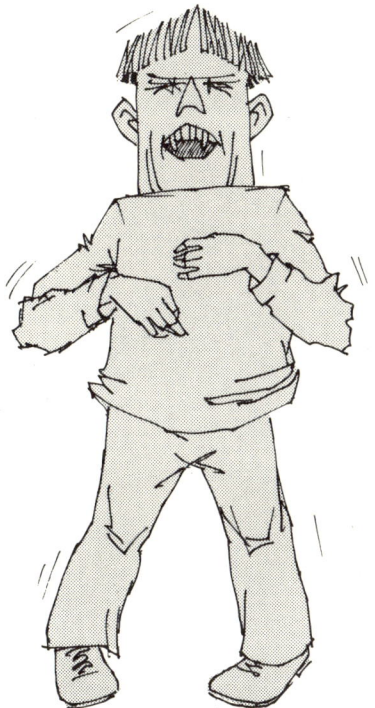

---
* See "Tricks, Shortcuts, Etcetera . . .", page 192.

THE TEACHER WILL NEED:

- a stapler

PREPARATIONS:

You will need tagboard (or other pattern-weight paperboard) patterns in the following sizes and dimensions:

- 6" × 12"
- Refer to illustrations

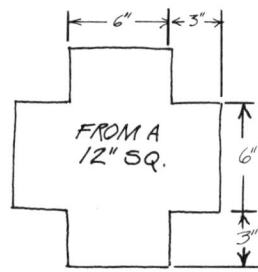
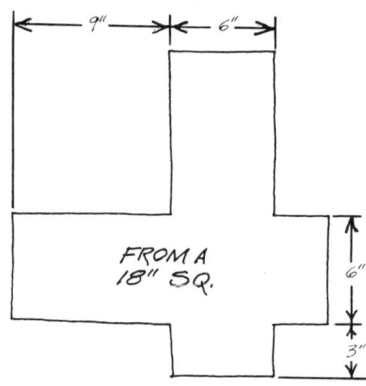

TO PRESENT:

1. Using your own work-along 18" × 24" sheet of construction paper as a visual aid, show your kids how to use the 6" × 12" paperboard as a *measuring strip** for penciling in the lines. Cut on the heavy lines.

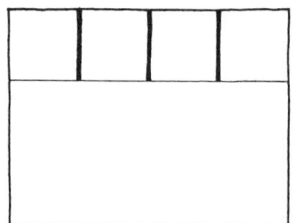

2. Explain that since this sheet of oversized paper will eventually fold up into a giant mask, it will be easier to work on the features while the mask is still flat. To this end, here are a few suggestions that your kids can put to good use:

Eyes: The "eyes" on a mask this large need not be functional because the wearer can always see out through the bottom of the mask or through an open mouth.

---

* See "Tricks, Shortcuts, Etcetera . . ." under Measuring Strips, Straightedges and Rulers (page 195).

Nose: The nose can be a simple paste-on, or it can be a three-dimensional nose. Here are a couple of suggestions towards solving the problems of constructing a three-dimensional nose:*

- A conical nose flanged at the bottom needs only an accommodating nose hole and a bit of paste to look like the one shown on the right.

- A triangular nose is easily constructed by following the wordless directions given here. In this case, however, the accommodating nose hole will have to be triangular, and the final product will look something like the one at the right.

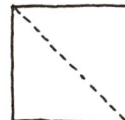 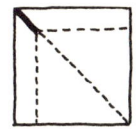 

Ears: To make a good all-around basic ear, all you need is a couple of ear-size scraps of paper folded as shown.

Then trim to taste, as suggested, and paste into position.

---

* However, it is my duty to point out to you that if you take this three-dimensional route, you may also have to allow for a generous amount of extra project time!

Hair: While hair can be as wild as brambles or as geometric as a well-tended hedge, there will always be those in your class who will be looking for something in a basic hair style. Here are a couple of good suggestions:

- *To Make Short Hair*: Have your kids trace the first pattern shown under *Preparations* onto a 12" square of construction paper, cut out the tracing, fold on the dotted lines, and fringe the hair as suggested here.

Assemble the basic mask and staple and secure the hair to the top with a dab or two of paste.

- *To Make Long Hair*: The only difference here between the long hair and short hair is the size of the sheet of paper. The long hair needs an 18" square of "hair" paper and the larger of the two patterns shown under *Preparations*.

But once you and your class are this far into the project—no further instructions will be necessary. Your kids will take over from here!

Lesson 8
Bag People

Anyone can crayon a couple of eyes onto a paper bag and mistakenly assume that they now know all there is to know about bag puppets; but the puppet that we are going to make here is to a paper bag what a symphony orchestra is to a tin whistle. In other words, if this is your first introduction to the *Bag People*, you have just bought yourself a front row seat to a first-class show!

EACH CHILD WILL NEED:

- a flat-bottom lunch bag
- construction paper in assorted sizes as needed
- paste, pencil, scissors and crayons

Curtain Raisers

TO PRESENT:

A piece of red construction paper is folded and custom fitted to the puppet's mouth. The top flap of the extended "mouth" is folded back to make the upper lip, the lips are shaped, and the finished product is inserted into place and secured with "denture cream" (paste), as shown here.

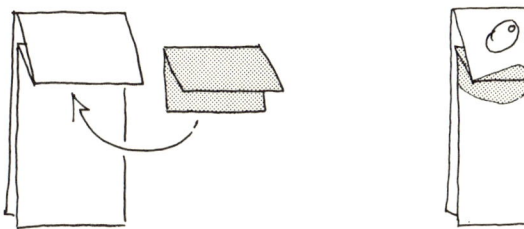

Then, given access to more construction paper and a little guidance in the principles of paper tailoring, your kids will take over from here!

Lesson 9
Pop Architecture

Pop Architecture is—by far—the best lesson of its kind that I have ever seen. Don't miss it!

EACH CHILD WILL NEED:

- practice paper
- drawing paper:
    6" × 15" and 6" × 9"
- 3" × 6" tagboard (or other pattern-weight paperboard (cut fractionally smaller on the 3" side),
- pencil, scissors, crayons (and possibly paste)

THE TEACHER WILL NEED:
- a stapler

PRACTICE EXERCISES:

As the Dean of the Classroom University, it will be your job to teach the foundation course in *Pop Architecture*. Here's what you'll need to know:

How to Make the Basic Pop-OUT

1. Fold a sheet of practice paper in half lengthwise and then make two cuts through the double thickness of paper to form "Flap A."

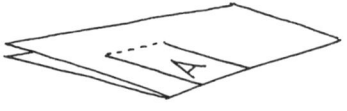

2. Fold up this flap and then fold back and repeat this swinging door exercise until the fold "loses its memory."

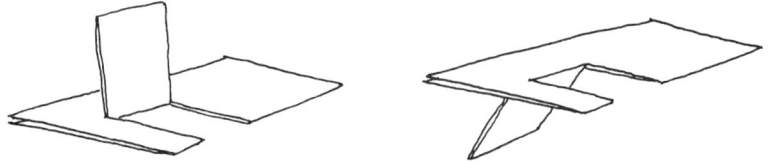

3. Now unfold the parent paper and activate the Pop-OUT.

Curtain Raisers

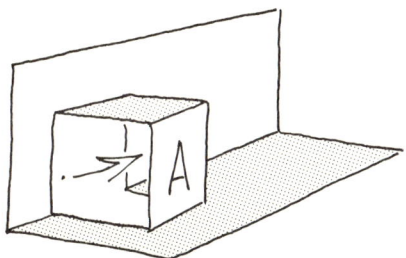

4. Once this principle is understood, skip a space and then make two more cuts as suggested here in Flap B, and continue as outlined above.

Got it? It's fun, it's easy, and your kids will love it!

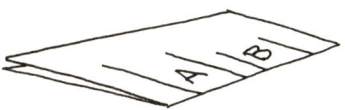

How to Make the Basic Pop-IN

The best way to explain a Pop-IN is to make one. Begin with a simple Pop-OUT and then add two more additional cuts as suggested. When both flaps have been exercised to lose their memories (see Step 2), push *out* the Pop-OUT and press *in* the Pop-IN to produce the architectural form shown here.

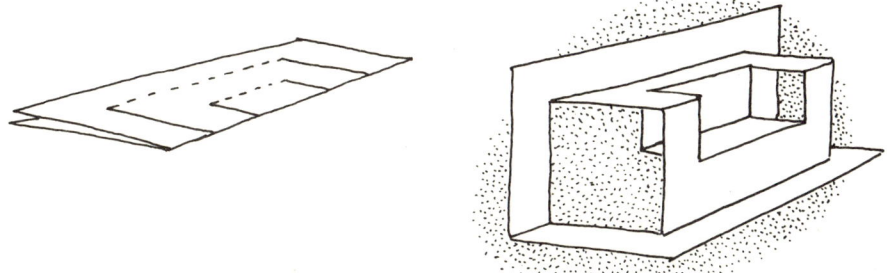

Super-Pops and How to Make Them

The figure at the left represents an activated Pop-OUT as seen from behind. The dotted lines represent the placement of a newly proposed "Flap B". The middle figure shows the same paper compressed to allow scissors to free the sides of Flap B. Once

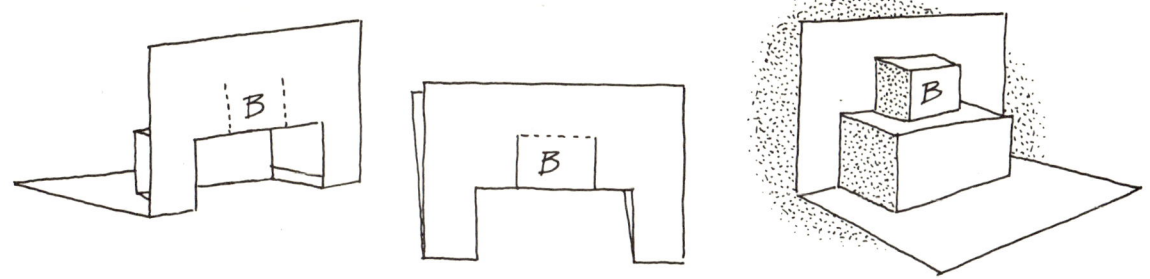

this new flap has been exercised and popped out, the resulting architectural form when seen from the front will look like the figure at the right.

A Confidence Test

Are you ready now for a trial architectural assignment? Then try this:

Using the same piece of practice paper that was used in the preceding exercise, see if you can add the penthouse and the entrance foyer shown here.

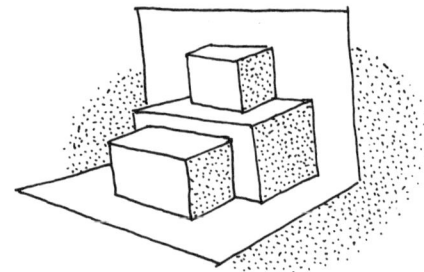

There—that wasn't so hard now, was it? And now that you understand "how to do it," you can begin to fully appreciate some of the creative possibilities that this lesson has to offer!

And the stand-up tree? (See illustration at the top of this lesson.) How was *that* done? Easy! It is simply a tree-shaped cut-out pasted onto an accommodating Pop-OUT. The same approach can also be used to create front view houses with peaked roofs, etc.

If it works—use it!

TO PRESENT:

1. Now that you have earned your doctorate in *Pop Architecture*, it is time to pass out the practice paper so that you can begin to share your excitement with your kids. Then—once they get the hang of it—pass out the 6" × 9" drawing paper and invite your young architects to build their own cities.

2. The display stands are made from the 6" × 15" paper, which is first folded in half lengthwise. Unfold and use the 3" × 6" tagboard as a *measuring strip** to draw the vertical lines. Fold on these lines and cut on the heavy lines. The final result is then folded up and stapled.

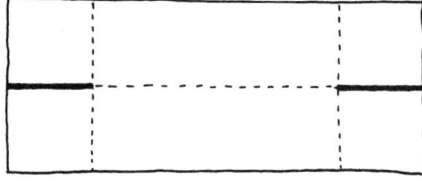 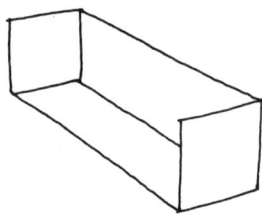

---

* See "Tricks, Shortcuts, Etcetera . . ." under *Measuring Strips, Straightedges and Rulers* (page 195).

Curtain Raisers

AND FINALLY:

When the cities are completed and decorated to taste, simply place them inside their tailor-made display stands and applaud!

Lesson 10
Dinner Plate Turkeys

I don't know what prompted me to invent this lesson, but I don't need an analyst to explain the natural affinity of turkeys to dinner plates.

After all—turkeys have to eat too!

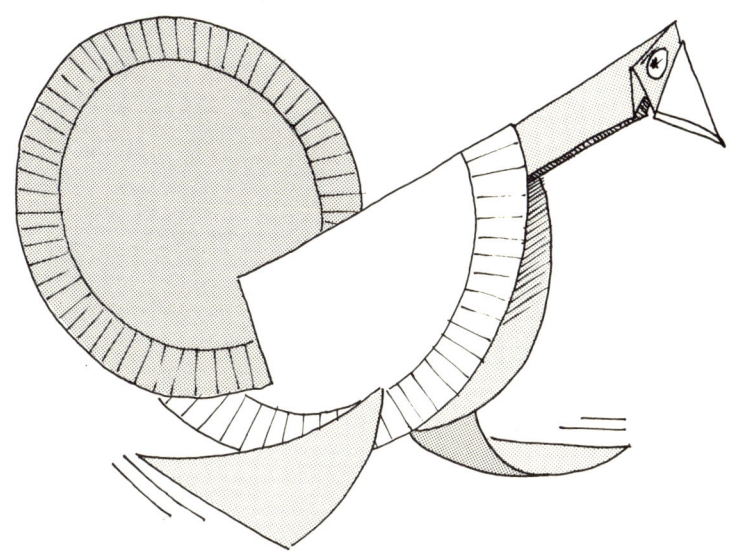

EACH CHILD WILL NEED:

- two 9" paper plates
- construction paper:
    - 2-1/4" × 6" red
    - 6" white square
    - 1-1/2" yellow square (and additional scraps of yellow as needed)
- scissors, crayons, and a small amount of paste

THE TEACHER WILL NEED:

- a stapler
- and either:
    - a single-edge razor blade (or hobby knife) and a sheet of cardboard
    - or a pair of heavy-duty scissors

TO PRESENT:

1. Have your kids paste their 1-1/2" yellow square to the end of their 2-1/4" × 6" red turkey necks. Add eyes and set to one side.

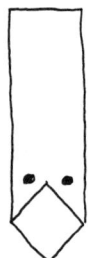

2. The plates are then turned upside down and crayoned in with some appropriate "turkey" color. The first of these turkey-colored plates is then folded in half and set off to one side to await the assembly instructions in Step 3.

3. Now, while all of this is going on, it is your job to invite your kids—one at a time—to bring their folded paper plates and their turkey necks to your desk so that you can staple turkey necks to turkey bodies and to use your razor blade or shears to cut a tail-slot into the turkey's back.

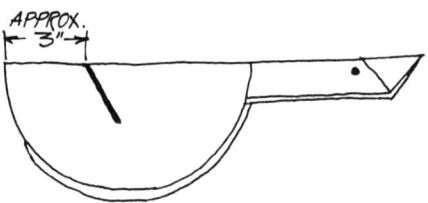

4. The white square is then cut on the diagonal, and the rest is easy: the wings are stapled to the bodies, the tailfeathers are inserted into the back, and the scraps of yellow construction paper are used to make the kernels of corn that will be needed to feed your noisy flock of hungry turkeys!

Lesson 11
Turkey Hats

You may think it's silly to wear a turkey on your head, and *I* may think it is silly to wear a turkey on my head; but put a turkey on a *child's* head and you have made an instant friend!

EACH CHILD WILL NEED:

- construction paper:
    12" × 18" gray and 9" square gray
    4-1/2" × 12" and 2-1/4" × 6" red
    1-3/4" yellow square
- paste, scissors and crayons

Curtain Raisers 49

THE TEACHER WILL NEED:
- a stapler

TO PRESENT:

1. Have your kids fold their 12" × 18" gray construction paper in half widthwise, unfold, and cut on the heavy lines as shown here.

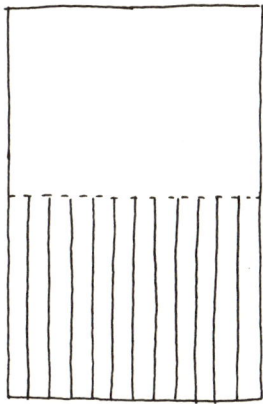

2. The 4-1/2" × 12" red paper is then folded in half lengthwise, unfolded, and the sides folded into the middle to divide the paper into four parts. Fold the turkey's

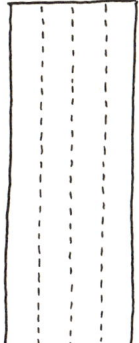 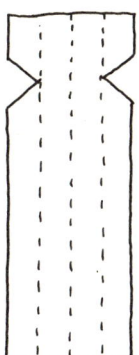 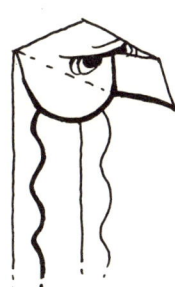

head as indicated by the dotted lines and unfold. Then cut a V-shaped notch on each side of this neck, paste on a yellow beak, add eyes, and trim the side flaps with a wiggly line, as suggested here. (The wiggly lines, however, should *not* touch the folded lines.)

3. Then while your kids are cutting their 9" squares into diagonal halves to make wings, your job is to staple the turkey necks, *Circlecone** the bodies, and staple.

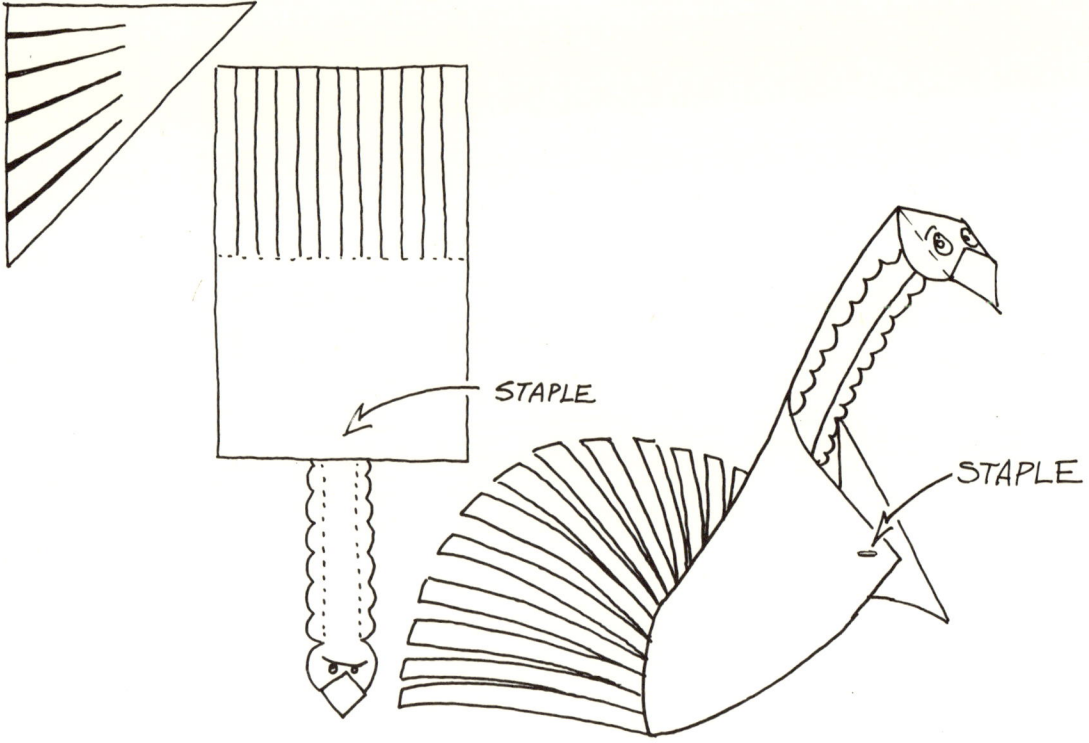

4. Add the wings and a tassel-like beard (from the 2-1/4" × 6" red), and it's all over but the gobble!

Turkey Hats? Your kids will love them!

Lesson 12
Turkey and Turkey Pilgrims

Here is one sure way to put the gobble back into your Thanksgiving celebration!

---

* See Tricks, Shortcuts, Etcetera . . ." (page 192).

Curtain Raisers

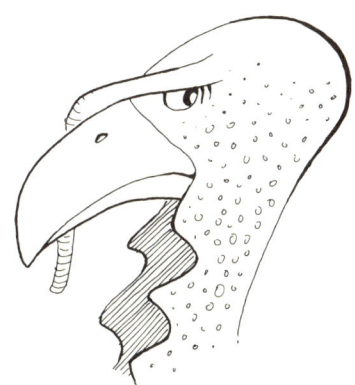

EACH CHILD WILL NEED:

- practice paper
- 12″ × 18″ drawing paper
- pencils and crayons

PREPARATIONS:

Basic Turkey-Drawing Instructions: If your knowledge of turkeys is as limited as mine, I suggest that you begin to familiarize yourself with the simple procedural steps shown here.

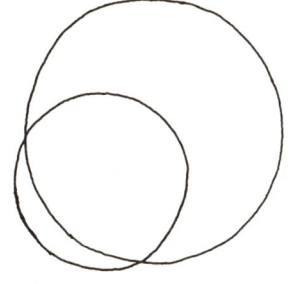  

TO PRESENT:

After giving your class a crash course in *Basic Turkey-Drawing*, suggest to your kids that they can put this knowledge to work in one of two ways: (1) that they create some kind of a true-to-life picture in which the turkey plays a primary role, or (2) that they make *Turkey-Pilgrims*.

"Turkey *what*?"

"*Turkey-Pilgrims*."

"What are *Turkey-Pilgrims*?"

Now that you have your kids where you want them, this is where the fun comes in! Explain that a *Turkey-Pilgrim* is either a turkey that looks like a Pilgrim or a Pilgrim that looks like a turkey. At this point, you can either show your kids the illustrations shown on page 52 or you can sketch a few *Turkey-Pilgrims* of your own on the chalkboard.* Either way, the presentation ends here and the creative part begins.

All you have to do from this point on is to pass out the art supplies and get out of the way. Your kids will do the rest!

---

* And if your drawing is "not very good"—that's all the better. What greater incentive could children have than the thought that their drawings might put their teacher's drawing to shame!

Lesson 13
There's No Place Like Home

This is the kind of lesson that gives teaching a good name. Try it and you'll see what I mean!

EACH CHILD WILL NEED:
- drawing paper:
    9" × 18"
    9" square

Curtain Raisers

- 4-1/2" or less × 9" tagboard (or other pattern-weight paperboard)
- pencils, scissors and crayons
- possibly paste

THE TEACHER WILL NEED:

- a stapler
- a single-edge razor blade or hobby knife, and a sheet of cardboard
- sufficient preparation time to review the material outlined in the introductory pages of the *Pop Architecture* lesson that begins on page 43.

TO PRESENT:

1. Begin by having your kids fold their 9" squares in half, then unfold and draw a table positioned as shown.

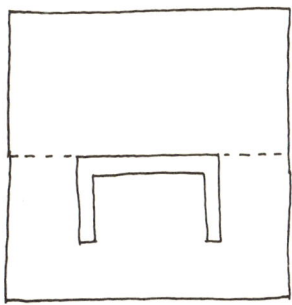

2. Once the tables have been drawn, have your kids refold their papers, turn their tables upside down, and cut on the heavy lines.

3. The table is then transformed into a *Pop-OUT* in exactly the same way as the buildings were handled in the *Pop Architecture* lesson. (See *How to Make the Basic Pop-OUT* instructions that begin on page 44.)

4. Now your job at this point is two-fold: (1) to use your razor blade to free the legs of the table and (2) to share the following instructions with your class.

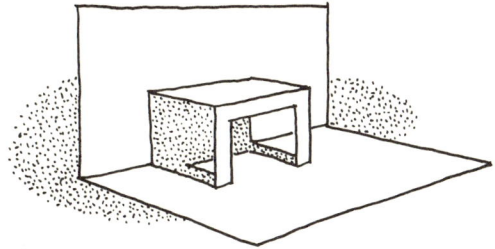

Pop-Out Chairs and How to Make Them

1. The chairs are drawn with their seat tops positioned on the center fold as shown here flanking a table.

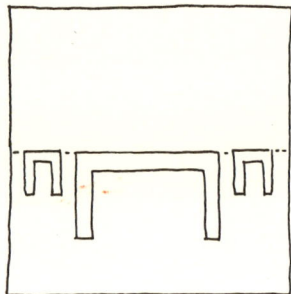

2. The chairs are then completed in one of two ways: either with their backs drawn on the adjoining wall or with an attached back.

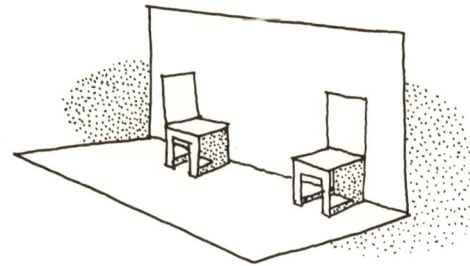

Other Homemaking Suggestions: The lesson on *Pop Architecture* (pages 43–47) is filled with ideas that can easily be adapted to this lesson.

Would you like a television set on your table? Or a pop-up toaster? Nothing could be easier! Or maybe you are just moving into a new apartment and would like to place a couple of boxes on the floor? With Pop-OUT technology, you can do all of these things—and more!

AND FINALLY:

Except for the size of the tagboard *measuring strip**, the instructions from this point on are identical to those given in the lesson in *Pop Architecture*.

To Make the Display Stand: Fold the 9" × 18" sheet of drawing paper in half lengthwise. Unfold and use the 4-1/2" × 9" tagboard strip to draw the vertical lines shown. Fold on these lines and cut on the heavy lines. The final result is then folded up and stapled.

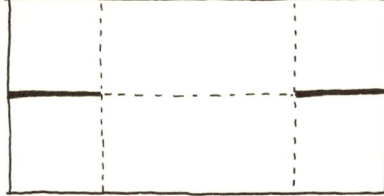 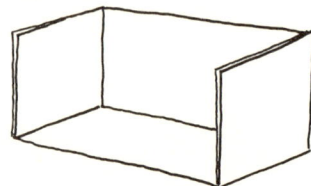

---

* See "Tricks, Shortcuts, Etcetera" (page 195).

Curtain Raisers 55

And when these rooms are finished and decorated to taste, simply place them into their display stands and secure with a couple of staples.

And that's *that*—enjoy!

Lesson 14
Raising a Pet Mouse

Some days may be good and some days may be better than good; but the day that you decide to introduce this *Pet Mouse* to your classroom will be a day that your kids will remember for years to come!

EACH CHILD WILL NEED:

- construction paper:
    - 4-1/2" × 6" brown and green
    - 2-1/4" × 3" white or gray
    - 2-1/4" × 3" yellow

THE TEACHER WILL NEED:

- a hand-held paper punch

TO PRESENT:

1. Using the *16-part box** fold and the 4-1/2" × 6" sheet of brown construction paper, have your kids assemble a box.

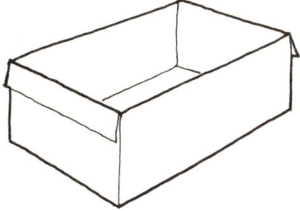

2. The 2-1/4" × 3" white or gray paper is folded in half widthwise and cut on this fold to divide the paper in half. One half of this paper is then used to make a *sail-*

---
* See "Tricks, Shortcuts, Etcetera . . ." under *Box Making* (Page 191).

boat cone* and the other part is cut up to make ears and a tail. The features are, of course, added with pencil or crayon.

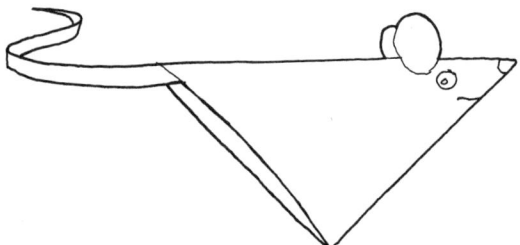

3. The green construction paper is then cut into narrow strips to make "grass" and then wrinkled to give the grass body.

4. The rest is easy. A hole is cut into one end of the bottom of the box and made large enough to accommodate the child's middle finger, the mouse is fitted onto the end of this finger, surrounded with "grass" and—presto! Each box will instantly give life to a wiggly mouse!

As your kids proudly carry their pets from desk to desk, it's your job to paper punch the small pieces of yellow paper until you have enough "Swiss cheese" on hand to feed an army of hungry mice!

Lesson 15
Santa with a Watermelon on His Head

One of the joys of teaching is the opportunity to watch a child's expression when a lesson takes an unexpected turn—and teaches by revelation.

(In other words, keep your eye on the "watermelon"!)

EACH CHILD WILL NEED:

- one-quarter of a paper plate and one-half of a paper plate
- construction paper:
    4-1/2" × 6" and 9" × 12" red

---

* See "Tricks, Shortcuts, Etcetera . . ." under *Sailboating* (page 198).

Curtain Raisers

3" × 4-1/2", 4-1/2" × 6", and 1-1/2" × 9" black
6" × 9" brown
1-1/2" square and a 3" square white
- paste, scissors and crayons

THE TEACHER WILL NEED:
- a stapler

TO PRESENT:

1. Have your kids color their "slice of watermelon" with a red crayon.

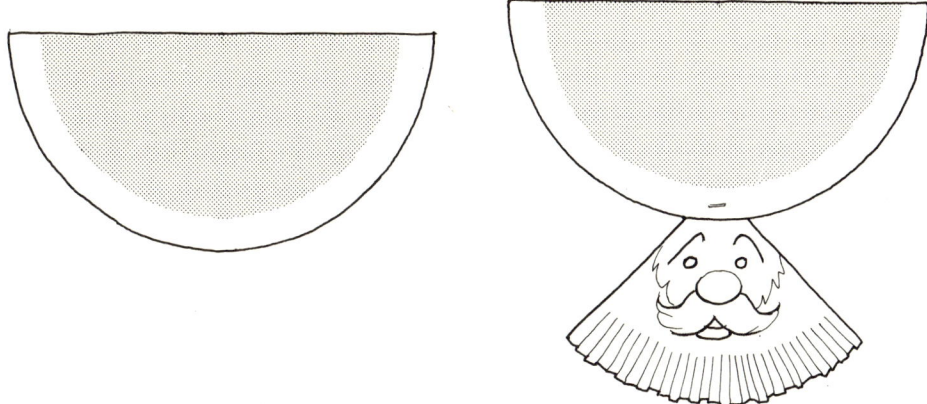

2. The one-fourth section of the paper plate is fringed along the curved edge to suggest a beard, finished Santa Claus style, and the "watermelon" is then stapled on top of Santa's head.

3. A circle is drawn on the 3" white square, cut out, fringed to make a pom-pom, and stapled onto the top of the "watermelon."

Now—up to this point, your kids will be both amused and perplexed ("What is Santa Claus doing with a *watermelon* on his *head*?")—but the moment of revelation comes when you staple the "watermelon" to the 9" × 12" red construction paper, *Circle-cone**, and staple again.

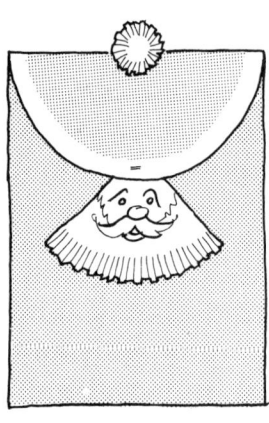 

4. The rest is easy. The 4-1/2" × 6" sheet of red construction paper is divided in half lengthwise to become the arms; the 4-1/2" × 6" black, to become the boots; the 1-1/2" × 9", the belt; and the white square, the buckle.**

---

* See "Tricks, Shortcuts, Etcetera . . ." (page 192).

** And by the way, the easiest way to make a buckle like the one shown here is not to cut out the center but simply to draw an interior square and to color it with a black crayon!

Curtain Raisers

AND FINALLY:

The 3" × 4-1/2" piece of black construction paper is divided in half lengthwise to make the gloves. And the 6" × 9" brown? Why it's just the right size to make a bag in which Santa can carry his presents!

Merry Christmas!

Lesson 16
Dashing Through the Snow

This is one of those lessons that cannot be recommended too highly. Your kids will love it—and so will you!

EACH CHILD WILL NEED:

- 9" × 18" white drawing paper and a 9" × 18" back-up sheet of (any color) drawing or construction paper, plus additional scraps as needed
- sleigh-colored construction paper:
    3" × 9", 6" × 11", and a 6" square
- shared patterns (see *Preparations* below)
- paste, pencil, scissors and crayons

THE TEACHER WILL NEED:

- a stapler

PREPARATIONS:

Using tagboard (or other pattern-weight paperboard), make a few *measuring strips** cut to the following sizes:

- 3" × 6"
- 4" × 6"
- 6" × 18"

---

* See "Tricks, Shortcuts, Etcetera . . ." (page 195).

Sleigh-Making Instructions

The Body: Using the 6" square of "sleigh-colored" construction paper, have your kids follow the instructions for making the *sixteen-part box** fold, cut off one strip of four squares and cut on the heavy lines. Fold and paste.

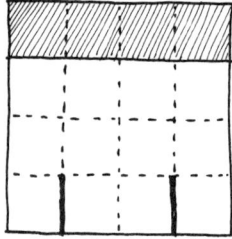 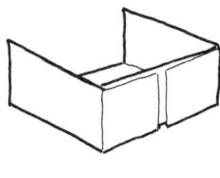

The Bed: Curl one end of the 3" × 9" strip of sleigh-colored construction paper and set aside for later.

The Runners: After advising your kids to press down firmly with their pencil points (so as to score the paper to make for easier folding) have them use their 3" × 6" and 4" × 6" *measuring strips** to lay out the 6" × 11" sleigh-colored sheet of construction paper, fold, curve the front runners, and paste the bottom flaps together.

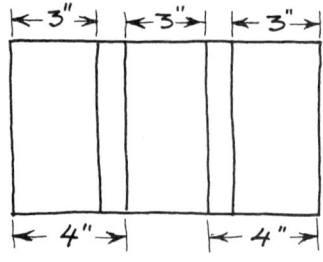 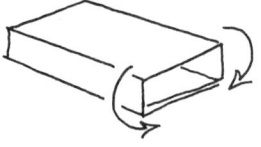 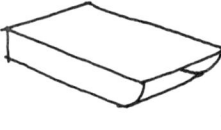

To Assemble the Sleigh: The body, the bed, and the runners are then pasted together.

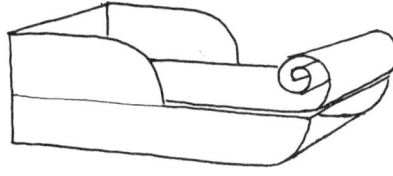

To Prepare the Snow for Sleighing

1. The 6" × 18" *Measuring Strips* are used for laying out the 9" × 18" white drawing paper as shown here.

---

* See "Tricks, Shortcuts, Etcetera" (page 191).

Curtain Raisers

2. Cut on these lines to within an inch or so of the opposite end of the paper. The runners of the sleigh are then threaded onto this newly formed center strip and the whole assembly stapled to the back-up sheet.

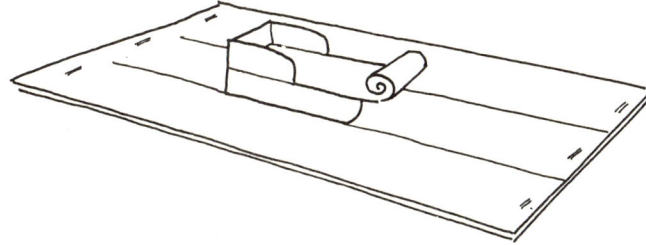

Further Suggestions: From here on out, turn this lesson over to your kids: let them celebrate the winter by filling their sleighs with passengers, presents, whatever!

And for those who will show an interest in learning how to make a convincing three-dimensional present, here's how:

1. Have your kids fold a square of paper using the *sixteen-part box** fold, remove a strip of 4 squares, cut on the heavy line, and paste.

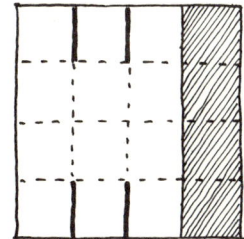 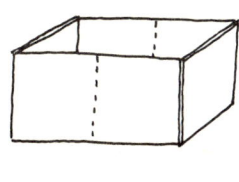

2. Cut as shown, and fold one side into the other. Then, using thin strips of construction paper as "ribbon," wrap well, attach a paper bow, and who could ask for more!

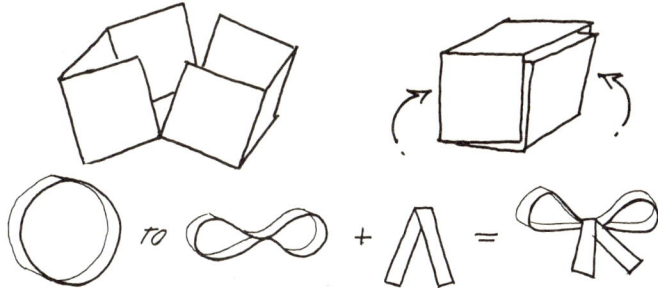

---

* See "Tricks, Shortcuts, Etcetera . . ." under *Box Making* (page 191).

Lesson 17
Super-Santa

Of all the Santa Claus ideas that have ever come out of my workshop, none has ever been greeted with more applause than this *Super-Santa*.

Try it—and you'll see what I mean!

EACH CHILD WILL NEED:

- white drawing paper:
    18" × 24", 4" × 18", 4-1/2" × 6", and a 4" square
    9" × 18" red construction paper
- paste, pencil, scissors and crayons

THE TEACHER WILL NEED:

- a stapler

TO PRESENT:

1. Have your kids fringe the 4" × 18" strip on each of the long sides. A circle cut from the 4" square is also fringed. Then both of these fringed pieces are pasted to the red paper as illustrated.

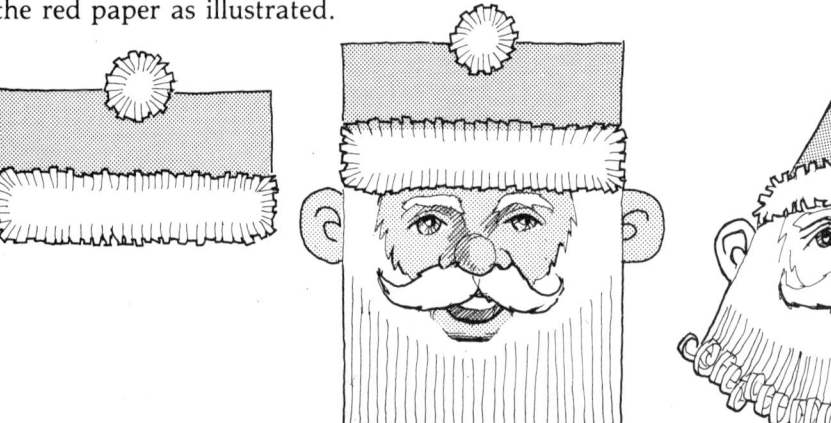

2. The red paper is, in turn, pasted to the 18" × 24" paper, Santa's face is drawn in and given a face tone,* and the 4-1/2" × 6" paper is given some of the same face tone and used for making a couple of ears—all as shown here.

3. The beard is then fringed with scissors and curled by rolling each beard strip on a pencil.

---

* At this point somebody is sure to raise a hand and ask, "So how do you make *skin* color?"

Most people have skin tones that can be approximated by a judicious mixture of red and browns. Some of us lean more towards the light reds (pinks) and some towards the browns, but—artistically speaking—none of us are *white* and none of us are *black*.

Curtain Raisers

AND FINALLY:

The finished Santa is *Circleconed* (see Tricks, Shortcuts, Etcetera . . .) and stapled, and the final product can either be worn as a mask or used as a decoration. Either way, it will be a classroom project remembered long after Christmas has come and gone!

Lesson 18
Reindeer Land!

My kids *loved* this lesson — *yours* will too!

EACH CHILD WILL NEED:

- 12" × 18" drawing paper
- 6" × 9" and a 6" square of brown construction paper
- a shared 3-1/2" (watercup size) circle pattern
- paste, pencil, scissors and crayons

TO PRESENT:

1. Have your kids use their circle pattern to trace half a circle onto their 6" × 9" brown paper.

2. Add nose, eyes, and highly-pitched antlers as suggested.

3. The 6" square of brown construction paper is for drawing the reindeer's body.

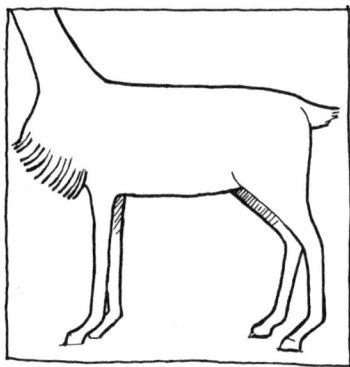

4. The head is then *Circleconed** and pasted, the two-part assembly is mounted onto the 12" × 18" drawing paper, and from this point on out, your kids will have their own ideas as to the many ways in which this reindeer can be put to good use!

Lesson 19
The World's Best Skating

This lesson is so good, I am willing to wager my last crayon that it will prove to be the best classroom skating party that you and your kids have *ever* attended!

EACH CHILD WILL NEED:

- white drawing paper:
    12" × 18"** and several 2-1/4" × 3"

---

* See "Tricks, Shortcuts, Etcetera . . ." (page 192).

** If this is going to be a roller skating lesson rather than an ice skating lesson, substitute an appropriate floor color.

Curtain Raisers 65

- 12" × 18" manila drawing paper
- pencil, scissors and crayons

THE TEACHER WILL NEED:

- a stapler
- a single-edge razor blade or hobby knife, and a 12" × 18" sheet of heavy cardboard

TO PRESENT:

1. Begin by having your kids use their 2-1/4" × 3" paper for drawing "a side-view skater standing on a block of ice."

2. Now, while your kids are hard at work drawing their figures, *you* have the job of stapling one of the short ends of the 12" × 18" white paper to the corresponding end of the 12" × 18" manila paper and of giving one of these double sheets to each of your young artists.

And once your kids have completed their figures, invite them to use their 12" × 18" white paper to plan their skating routes in pencil.

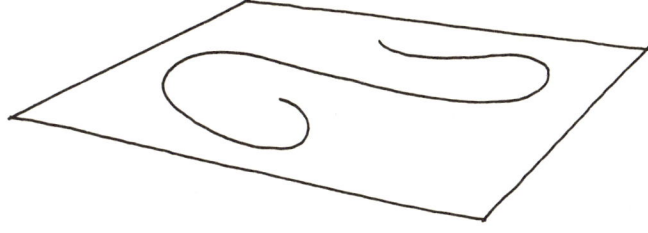

3. Meanwhile, there is one more job that has to be done: the figures must be cut out and their block-like pedestal cut up the middle. When this has been completed, have your kids turn up one side of the base flap in one direction and the other side in the other direction.

4. Now comes the special "magic" that transforms this lesson into something very special:

Having your kids line up at your desk—one at a time—you slip your sheet of heavy cardboard between the white paper and the back-up sheet and use your razor blade to slit the paper along the pre-penciled routes.

Now once the routes have been slit, the base tabs of the skaters are placed through the slits *so that the stand-up skaters can actually "skate" along these pre-planned skating routes.**

5. Needless to say, once your kids begin to see the inherent possibilities of this concept, the excitement will inspire the creation of everything from ice shows to hockey games with stand-up nets!

Lesson 20
Snow Hill

Here is another good way to get a rise out of your class—and your kids will enjoy every minute of it!

EACH CHILD WILL NEED:

- white drawing paper:
    6" × 18" and 12" × 18"

---

* Since it is impossible for these (or any other skaters) to take sharp, angular turns, your job may also entail taking liberties with some of the more erratic pre-planned routes!

Curtain Raisers

- 4-1/2" × 6" manila drawing paper
- 3" × 4-1/2" construction paper in assorted bright colors (and small scraps of matching colors)
- shared tagboard (or other pattern-weight paperboard.):
  2-1/4" × 4-1/2" and 4" × 18" *measuring strip**

THE TEACHER WILL NEED:

- a stapler

TO PRESENT:

1. Begin by having your kids use their 4-1/2" × 6" paper to draw a standing figure. This figure should be dressed for a day in the snow and be standing—arms at side—as suggested here. This figure is then completed in crayon, cut out with scissors, and turned over and finished on the reverse side as well.

---

* See "Tricks, Shortcuts, Etcetera . . ." (page 195).

2. The 2-1/4" × 4-1/2" measuring strips are used for laying out the 3" × 4-1/2" colored construction paper sleds. Fold on these lines, curve the front runners and, from another scrap of paper, add a steering bar.

 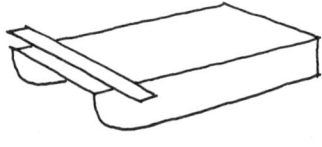

3. The 4" × 18" measuring strips are used to lay out the 12" × 18" white drawing paper. Cut on the heavy lines and fold up and paste.

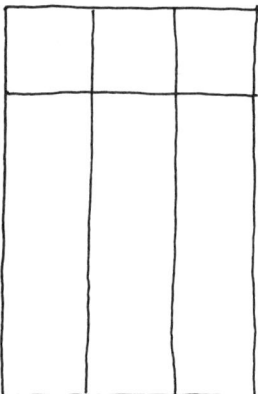 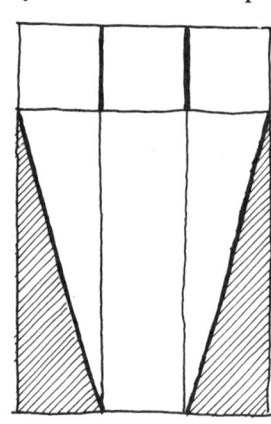 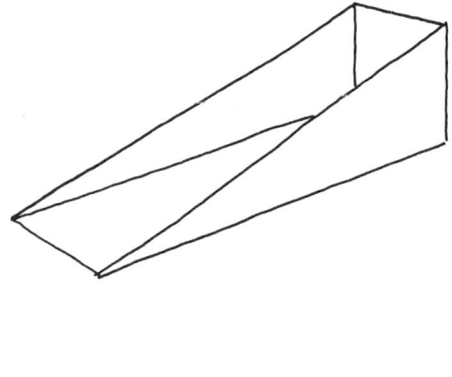

4. And the rest is easy! The figures are pasted onto the sleds, and the 6" × 18" white paper is stapled to the "top of the hill" as shown here.

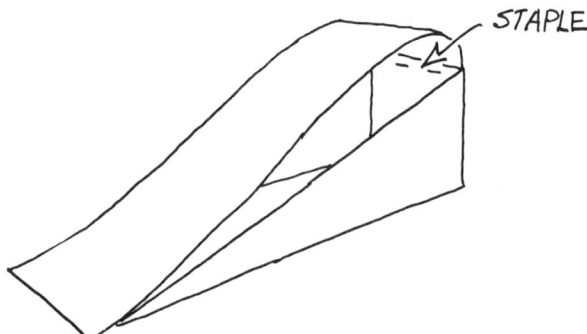

AND FINALLY:

Once your kids experience the first thrill of taking their homemade sleds "down the hill", your job will be to keep them supplied with paper, for your classroom hills will soon become popular with coasters and skiers alike!

Skiers? How do you make skiers?

Your kids will find a way!

Curtain Raisers 69

Lesson 21
Dancin' for the Fun of It!

Here is an easy-to-make classroom entertainer who can dance to all the latest tunes. Enough said!

EACH CHILD WILL NEED:

- 6" × 12" drawing paper
- 8-1/2" (+ or −) square of newsprint (or other inexpensive paper)
- 2 small paperclips
- pencils, scissors and crayons

THE TEACHER WILL NEED:

- a roll of tape

TO PRESENT:

1. Since this lesson will turn the spotlight onto the world of dance, explain to your kids that the sooner they decide on the "who" of this matter, the more fun this is going to be for everyone. ("Who is this going to be? Is this going to be someone who is going to dance on a stage or a street corner? Is this a musician, a party-goer, a performance artist . . . ? *You're* the agent—*you* decide!")

2. And since this lesson is also an excellent way to introduce the concept of proportions, have your kids fold their 6" × 12" drawing papers in half lengthwise to establish the basic symmetry of the human body, and in half widthwise to determine the proportional length of the legs. And for reasons that will soon become evident, have your kids draw their figures on tiptoes, legs together.

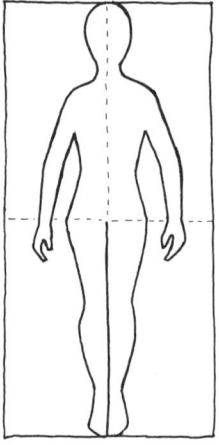
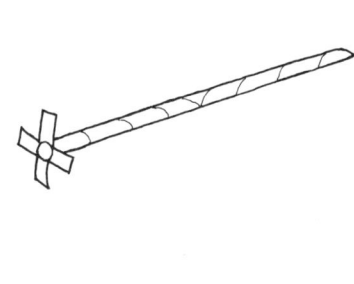

Now, while your kids are busy putting the finishing touches on their figures and cutting them out with scissors, *your* job is to distribute a short length of tape (no more than 5 inches) to each participant.

3. The squares of newsprint are then rolled into *paper straws** and secured with a small snippet of tape. Once secured, have your kids use their scissors to splay one end of this paper straw.

4. The dancer's feet are now folded out into a normal standing position and a paper-clip "tap" is attached to each foot. Then—after folding at the elbows, wrists and knees—the show is nearly ready to begin!

5. Have your kids cut their tape in half and to use these pieces to secure the splayed ends of the paper straw to the back of the dancer.

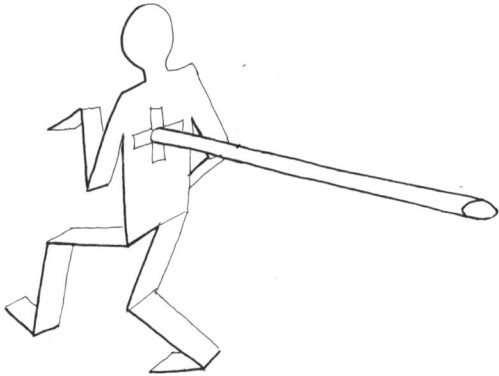

And that's it! Turn on the music, stand back—and enjoy!

---
* See "Tricks, Shortcuts, Etcetera . . ." (pages 197–198).

Curtain Raisers   71

Lesson 22
Traveling in the Fast Lane

From a kid's point of view, this lesson is almost as much fun as being old enough to borrow the keys to the family car!

EACH CHILD WILL NEED:

- construction paper:
    6" × 9" assorted "car colors" (see *Preparations* below)
    12" × 18" gray
- pencil, scissors and crayons

THE TEACHER WILL NEED:

- a stapler

PREPARATIONS:

The 6" × 9" car papers are prefolded to the dimensions given below. (The easiest way that I have found to cut this preparation time down to a minimum is to do all my folding against the metal edge of my papercutter. Not only does this help to speed up the folding, but the ruled lines of the papercutter supply the perfect answer to all of the dimensioning requirements!)

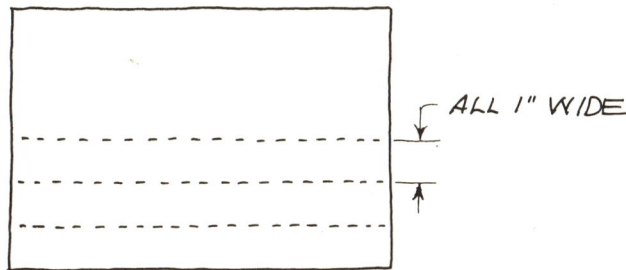

TO PRESENT:

1. Explain to your kids that, for reasons that will soon become evident, the basic lines of their cars must be drawn to the following specifications:

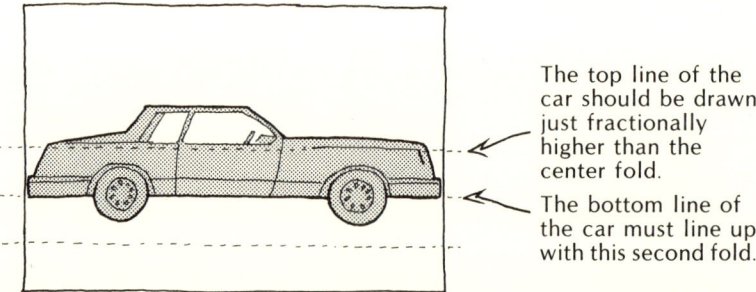

The top line of the car should be drawn just fractionally higher than the center fold.

The bottom line of the car must line up with this second fold.

2. Once the cars (station wagons, pickup trucks, etc.) have been drawn to these basic specifications, cut away the shaded areas indicated and cut on all heavy lines.

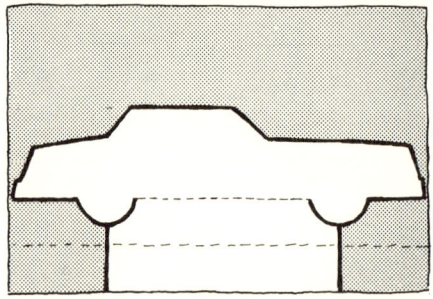

3. The flap is then folded up against the back and secured at the top with a couple of staples.

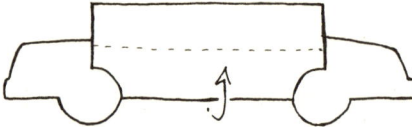 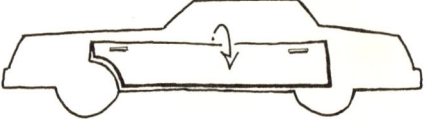

4. One of the long edges of the 12" × 18" gray paper is then folded up and secured to each end with a staple.

AND FINALLY:

Once your kids understand that the folded flap of gray is the road on which their cars are free to travel, *your* part in this lesson is over. The background will take care of itself! (For one suggestion, see the illustration at the top of page 71.)

Curtain Raisers 73

Lesson 23
A Basket Filled with Love

Decorate it with hearts, fill it with flowers, or load it with Christmas cookies—here is truly a basket for all seasons.

EACH CHILD WILL NEED:

- colored construction paper:
    12" square, 3" × 18" and extra sheets as needed
- a shared pattern (see *Preparations*)
- scissors

THE TEACHER WILL NEED:

- a stapler

PREPARATIONS:

Using tagboard (or other pattern-weight paperboard), make a few 11-1/2" doughnut-shaped patterns, as shown here.

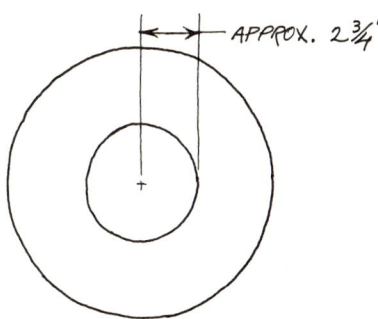

TO PRESENT:

1. Have your kids trace their patterns onto the 12" square of colored construction paper.

While pattern-tracing and cutting can hardly be ranked among the world's most difficult assignments (especially when one child holds while the other traces), this particular assignment comes with important DOs and DON'Ts: 1) press down firmly with the pencil point when tracing the inside circle, and 2) *don't* cut out the center of the traced "doughnut".

2. Once the outside edge of this traced pattern is cut out, have your kids place a dot in the center, and draw a line from this dot to the outside rim, and cut on this line.

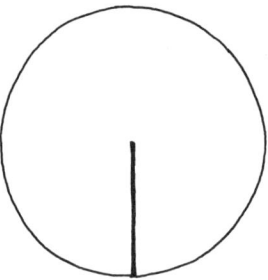

3. Now comes the part of the instructions that is far easier to show by example than to describe in words; so I suggest that you take time to master this next maneuver before you attempt to explain it to your class! In short, here is what happens and why:

Since the heavy-handed tracing of the inner circle has scored* the fibers of the paper, this inner circle can now be folded. And once folded, it can be overlapped and stapled.

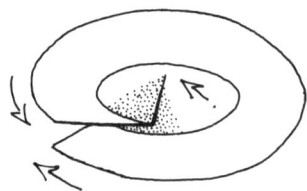 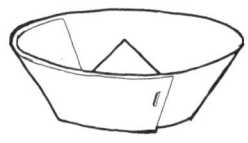

AND FINALLY:

The 3" × 18" strip is folded lengthwise to become the handle, and the handle is, in turn, stapled to the basket.

Enjoy!

Lesson 24
Weaving with a Wobble

You probably have seen variations of this lesson done elsewhere but never have had the courage to attempt it on your own.

Now, thanks to the detailed procedural steps that follow, here is a failproof lesson plan that finally takes the worry out of the wobble!

---

* See "Tricks, Shortcuts, Etcetera . . ." under *Scoring* (page 200).

Curtain Raisers

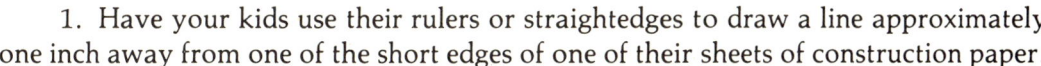

EACH CHILD WILL NEED:

- two sheets of 9" × 12" construction paper in contrasting colors
- a shared ruler or straightedge
- pencil, scissors and paste

TO PRESENT:

To Make the Warp

1. Have your kids use their rulers or straightedges to draw a line approximately one inch away from one of the short edges of one of their sheets of construction paper.

2. From the center of this ruled line to the center of the opposite side of the paper, have your kids draw a wavy line as suggested here.*

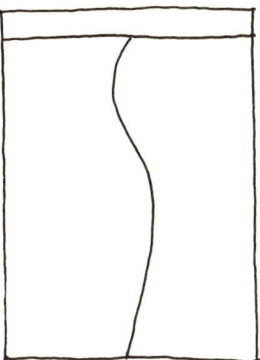

---

* Caution your kids to make sure that none of these lines double back as shown here.

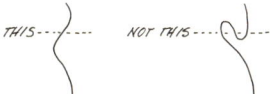

3. Then draw two more wavy lines.

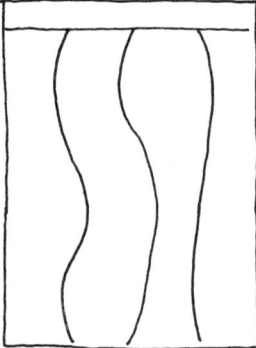

4. And finally, after cautioning your kids not to make any of these strips too narrow, have them draw four more lines. Cut on all wavy lines.

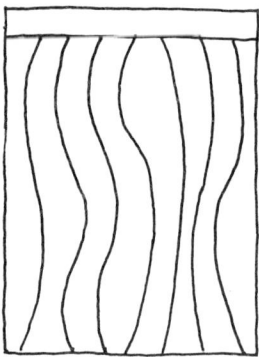

To Make the Woof

On the second sheet of colored construction paper have your kids use their pencils to draw ten or eleven wavy lines across the width of their paper and to lightly number these strips at both ends.

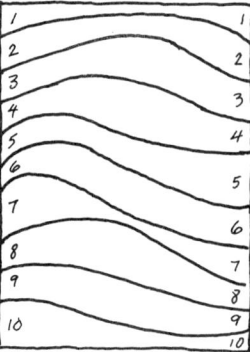

Curtain Raisers

To Weave

1. The rest is easy. Beginning with woof strip 1, have your kids cut off *one* strip at a time and weave!

2. And when the warp is filled, paste down the loose ends, trim, and display with pride!

Lesson 25
Seeing Through It All

Tired of square-cornered classroom dioramas? Then take heart and come 'round—for this lesson will convincingly demonstrate how a superior illusion can lie just around the corner!

Read on and you'll see *exactly* what I mean!

EACH CHILD WILL NEED:

- drawing paper:
    6" × 9"
    6" × 12" *or* 9" × 12" (see Step 2 on page 78)
- pencil, scissors and crayons

THE TEACHER WILL NEED:

- a stapler

PREPARATIONS:

The best way to present this lesson is to prepare a mock-up of your own to show your kids. So skip ahead to see what's coming, and then get down to work. The figure to the left represents the front of the foreground sheet (with the shaded part removed); the figure to the right, the reverse side of this same sheet.

 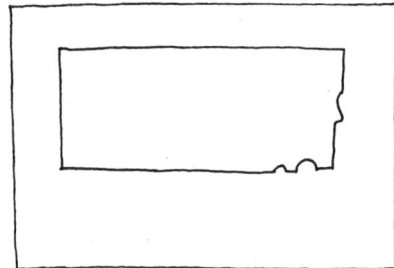

TO PRESENT:

1. Pass out the 6" × 9" drawing paper and explain to your kids that the diorama they are about to make will differ considerably from other dioramas they may have made in the past.

"For starters," you say, as you hold up your prepared visual aid, "the foreground might look something like this." At that, you turn your visual aid *back-to* so that your kids can see what they are going to be dealing with, which—when reduced to its lowest common denominator—is actually nothing more than a hole in a sheet of paper!

Turning the visual aid *front-to* again, you explain that the cut-away portion could be designed to represent an opening in a forest, an entrance to a cave, the cabin of an alien spacecraft, or any of a thousand and one other equally satisfactory ideas.*

And once your kids grasp the concept, let them go to work!

2. As your kids are hard at work preparing their foreground sheets, it's your job to keep one jump ahead by preparing your own background sheet:

---

* For some kids (especially younger kids who might be easily confused by the idea of "an opening in a forest"), this lesson is best presented as a window lesson "looking out."

Curtain Raisers

If your foreground is horizontal in format, your background will be 6" × 12"; if vertical, 9" × 12". Whatever the size, fold in the sides of the background paper and unfold. It is important to note that, with the exception of the narrow side flaps which are used for stapling, this *entire* second sheet becomes the background.

When ready, assemble your background to your foreground and display so that your kids can "get the idea". Then hand out the background sheets and let your kids get back to work!

Further Presentation Suggestions: One of the wonderful features of this lesson is the way that this diorama can loan itself to exploring the mysteries of the parallax—for, just as in nature, the slightest movement of the viewer's head will cause an apparent displacement in the relationship between objects in the background and those in the foreground.

And once the consciousness of your kids has been raised to appreciate this phenomenon—their world will never be the same!

Lesson 26
World's Ugliest Trolls and Leprechauns

I've seen some ugly creatures in my life, but *none* as ugly as these—your kids will love them!

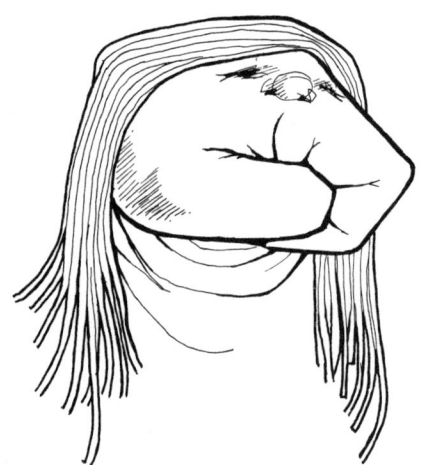

EACH CHILD WILL NEED:

- 9" × 12" drawing paper
- shared patterns and a portion of yarn (see *Preparations*)
- pencil, scissors and crayons

THE TEACHER WILL NEED:

- a container of glue
- a black marker (water-soluble)
- 9" × 12" tagboard (or other pattern-weight paperboard)
- a single-edge razor blade or hobby knife, and a desk-protecting sheet of cardboard

PREPARATIONS:

Pattern-Making Instructions: Using the 9" × 12" sheet of tagboard and the guidelines below, prepare oval patterns as suggested.

Approximate Oval Sizes		
	height	width
first grade size:	1-1/2"	2-5/8"
third grade size:	1-3/4"	3"
adult:	2"	3-1/2"

Curtain Raisers

You will need adult pattern for yourself, and a few child-size patterns for classroom sharing.

Preparing the Yarn: Since the yarn is to become the creature's hair, each child will need a wig's worth!

The way to cut measured lengths with ease is to wrap the yarn around a solid object—such as a book, a piece of cardboard, etc.—so that you can cut a handful at a time. (Approximately ten strands of heavy yarn per person should be enough.)

TO PRESENT:

1. Have your kids use the patterns to trace the right size oval onto their drawing paper. Once the oval has been traced, invite your kids to poke a hole into the center of the oval, cut out the interior with scissors, and discard.

2. The rest is easy! Reserving the oval-shaped hole for the creature's head, invite your kids to complete the rest of the picture as suggested here.

3. The glue is for the yarn, the yarn is for the hair, and the marker is for drawing eyes and nose on the clenched fist of each artist.

Enjoy!

Lesson 27
Salted Eggs

To watch kids at work on this lesson is to understand why you chose to become a teacher!

EACH CHILD WILL NEED:

- 12" × 18" drawing paper
- pencil and crayons

THE TEACHER WILL NEED:

- one 3" × 4" sheet of stiff paper
- one sheet 4-1/2" × 6" tagboard (or other pattern-weight paperboard)
- a pointed stylus (the handle of a watercolor brush, the business end of a knitting needle, or anything else that will do the job described in *Preparations*.)
- pencil and scissors

PREPARATIONS:

1. Using the 3" × 4" paper, cut out a large egg.* Trace this egg onto the center

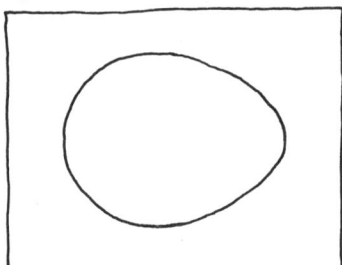

---

* For assistance in this matter, consult "Tricks, Shortcuts, Etcetera . . ." under *Eggs and Ovals* (page 193).

ot the tagboard. Cut away the inside of this egg drawing so as to leave an egg-shaped hole in the middle of the tagboard.

2. Using your stylus and the egg-shaped hole as your pattern, trace three eggs onto the lower portion of each sheet of 12" × 18" drawing paper as suggested here.

3. And now that I have coaxed you this far, let's see if I can talk you into one more classroom preparation:

To make the *perfect* presentation, you should really forget about your kids for a few minutes and give some thought to preparing a *Salted Eggs* picture of your own. While this step is not absolutely necessary to the success of this lesson, effort expanded here will be promptly repaid with compound interest!

And with *that*—your preparations are over and your presentation is ready to begin

TO PRESENT:

1. Pass out the prepared sheets of 12" × 18" drawing paper without comment so that your kids can be the first to discover the hidden eggs. Once this whispered news has traveled the room, invite your class to use their pencils to outline these eggs on *both* sides of the drawing paper.

2. Decorate the eggs on one side of this paper only.

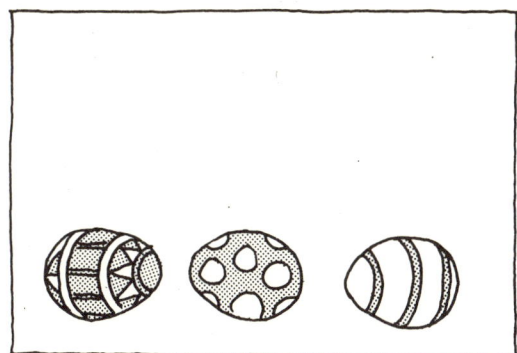

3. Now (provided that you have been able to find time to prepare a Salted Eggs picture of your own), the fun part of the presentation is about to begin.

Having secretly placed *your* completed picture on top of a couple of sheets of unprepared paper, you turn off the classroom lights and walk over to the window.

"Here is how it works," you announce. " 'Look at my picture of decorated Easter eggs', you say to your mother." At this point you hold up the stack of papers with your finished picture displayed on top.

" 'What *decorated* Easter eggs?' " your Mother asks. " 'I don't see any *decorated* Easter eggs. All I see are *white* eggs!' "

" 'Then I guess I had better color them!' " you say as you hold your picture up to the window and whip away the backing.

And with *that*—the white eggs will immediately transform themselves into radiantly backlighted masterpieces worthy of a young Faberge!

4. Even after the secret is out, do not assume that all of your kids will understand what they have seen, but once you take the pains to see that all of the papers get turned over before the second part of this lesson begins, *your* job is over.

Congratulations!

Lesson 28
An Egg-Bearing Rabbit

Some lessons come with their own special kind of magic—and *this* is one of those lessons!

Curtain Raisers

EACH CHILD WILL NEED:

- white or manila drawing paper:
  one 6" × 12", 3" × 18", 6" × 9"
  one 9" square
  two 3" × 9"
- a shared pattern (see *Preparations* below)
- paste, pencil, scissors and crayons

PREPARATIONS:

Using tagboard (or other pattern-weight paperboard), make the following:

- 7-inch circle
- an egg-shaped pattern* suitable for tracing onto a sheet of 6" × 9" drawing paper

TO PRESENT:

1. Have your kids trace the egg pattern onto the 6" × 9" drawing paper. These traced eggs are then cut out and decorated.

2. The 7-inch circle pattern is then traced onto the 9-inch square and cut out to become the rabbit's head. The 3" × 9" papers are, of course, for the ears.

3. To make the body, have your kids fold their 6" × 12" paper into quadrants and cut on the heavy line. Once the rabbit's legs have been freed, have your kids turn up the feet—and with that, you now have your armless rabbits ready for assembly.

---

* For help in preparing this pattern, see "Tricks, Shortcuts, Etcetera . . ." under Eggs and Ovals (page 193).

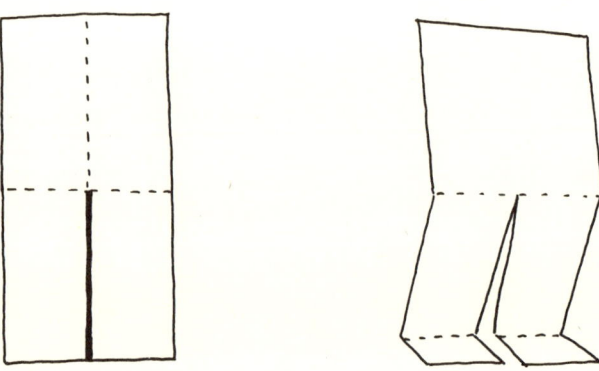

4. After the heads are attached to the bodies and the rabbits are dressed (or colored au naturel), the 3" × 18" arm unit is pasted or stapled on from behind.

AND FINALLY:

The decorated egg is attached to either one or both of the paws! Enjoy!

Lesson 29
How Does Your Garden Grow?

To help you celebrate the end of winter, here is a pair of springtime lessons in full bloom. Enjoy!

Curtain Raisers

Activity 1: A Beginner's Bouquet

EACH CHILD WILL NEED:

- 12" × 18" drawing paper
- construction paper:
    - 6" × 9" assorted "vase" colors
    - 3" × 4-1/2" assorted "flower" colors
    - 6" × 12" green
- paste, pencil, scissors and crayons

THE TEACHER WILL NEED:

- a desk stapler with about a 4-inch stapling throat

TO PRESENT:

1. Have your kids fold their 6" × 9" "vase" paper in half lengthwise, draw a snake-like line down the "open" side, and cut as suggested.

2. Unfold and decorate.

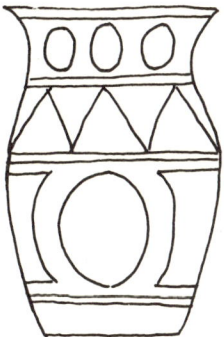

3. *Your* job at this point is to use your desk stapler to secure the upper corners of each vase to the 12" × 18" background paper, and to encourage your kids to cut long stems from the green paper. The stems are then inserted into the vases and pasted at their top ends as suggested here.

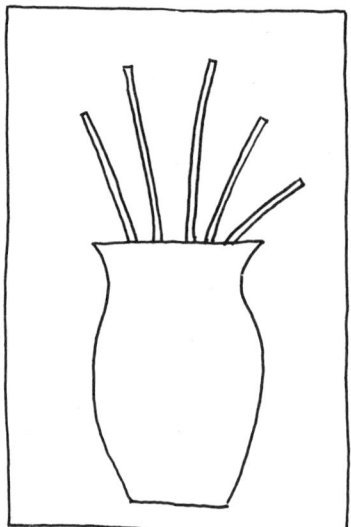

4. The smaller pieces of colored paper are for the flowers, the remainder of the green paper is for the leaves, the bottom of the vase is pasted to the background paper, and—with that—spring has officially arrived!

Activity 2: A Bouquet with a Difference

EACH CHILD WILL NEED:

- construction paper:
    12" × 18" background sheet
    4-1/2" × 6" assorted "flower" colors
    3" × 12" green
- 6" × 9" white drawing paper
- paste, pencil, scissors and crayons

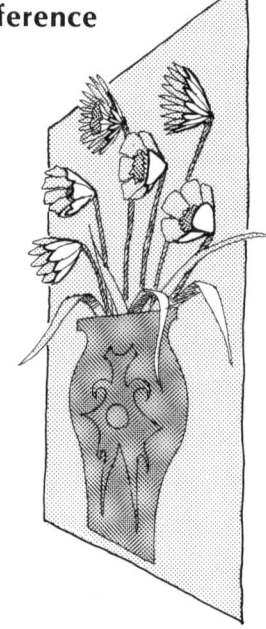

Curtain Raisers

THE TEACHER WILL NEED:

- a roll of tape
- a single-edge razor blade or a hobby knife, and a desk-protecting sheet of cardboard

PREPARATIONS:

Using the razor blade or hobby knife and the cardboard, cut out five or more one-half inch square holes in each sheet of the 12" × 18" background paper, as suggested here.

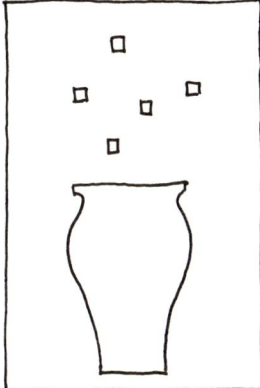

TO PRESENT:

1. Begin as in the previous lesson, but this time, *paste* the green leaves to the back of the vase, *paste* the vase to the background paper, and draw in the stems as shown.

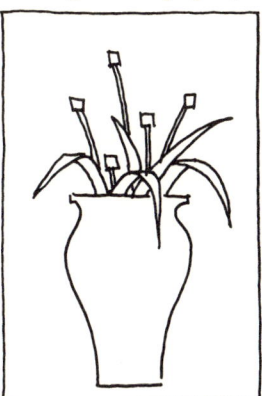

2. Now explain to your kids that—for reasons that will soon become evident—all flowers must be drawn on the "flower papers" inside a lightly penciled circle.

3. Once the flowers have been drawn and cut out with scissors, have your kids place a dot in the center of each flower and cut to the dot as suggested by the dark line. The flowers are then *circleconed** and pasted as shown.

4. Now comes the part that raises this lesson considerably above other flower lessons: after giving each child a length of tape (maybe 5 inches or so), invite your kids to turn their papers over and place a short length of tape over each hole. Then turn back to the front again and apply the back end of the flowers to the tape where they'll "stick like magic!"

Further Suggestions: More elaborate flower forms can be made by making the flowers in two parts as suggested here. Note that the outer part of this alternate flower form is made with a "doughnut hole."

To attach this two-part flower to the background paper, simply press the center of the flower through the "doughnut hole" of the surrounding petals, and press to the exposed tape as explained in the cutaway diagram shown here.

Now—stand back and applaud!

---

* See "Tricks, Shortcuts, Etcetera . . ." (page 192).

Curtain Raisers

Lesson 30
A Flat-Bottom Boat for All Occasions

This flat-bottom boat is easy to make and is filled with creative possibilities. Enjoy it!

EACH CHILD WILL NEED:

- construction paper:
    - 12" square "boat colored"
    - 12" square of blue "water"
- 4-1/2" × 6" drawing paper
- paste, pencil, scissors and crayons

TO PRESENT:

1. Have your kids fold their 12-inch square of "boat" paper into 16 parts as shown here, cut off the shaded portion, and save both pieces.

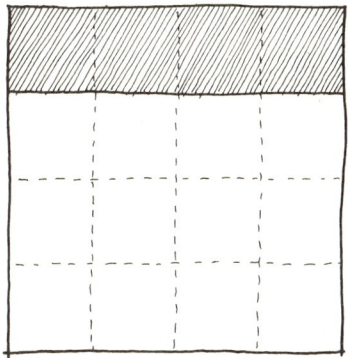

2. Fold the long sides of the longer piece. Unfold. Cut off the shaded areas as shown and cut on all heavy lines. Again—save all pieces!

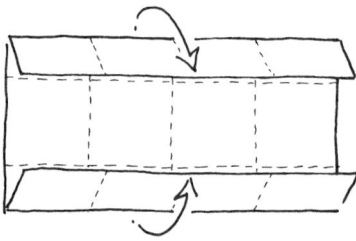 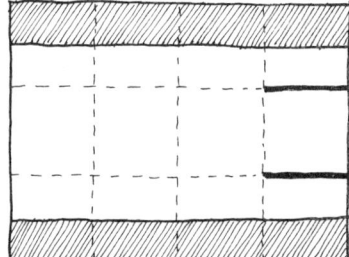

3. Have your kids draw lines A-B and A-C as indicated and cut on the heavy lines and fold on the dotted lines.

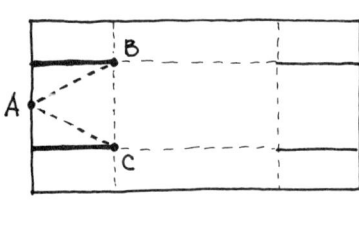 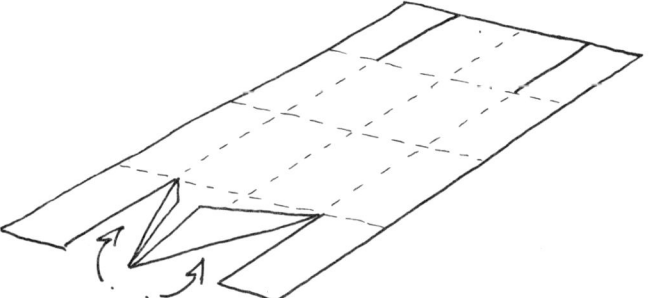

4. And with that, your fleet of flat-bottom boats will be ready for the assembly line!

To Assemble the Stern: Fold up the side flaps and secure same with the enveloping back flap.

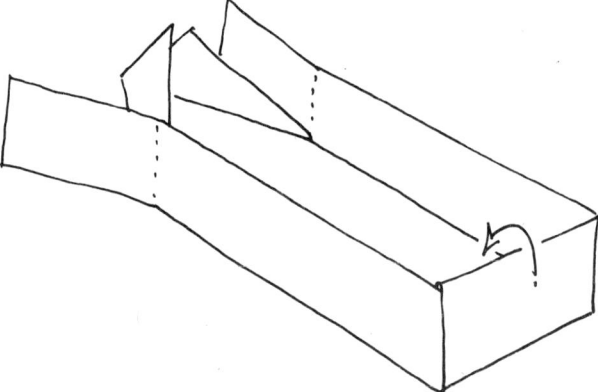

To Assemble the Bow: Paste the sides of the boat to the upraised triangular flaps. Since the assembled bow will come up a little short on material, you will have to show your kids how to remedy this situation using a little paste and part of a ready-made scrap left over from step 2. Now, all that is left to do is to make seats (see Step 3, *Getting into Deep Water*, pages 31 and 32) and to add the necessary personal touches that will give the boat its suggested character.

Curtain Raisers

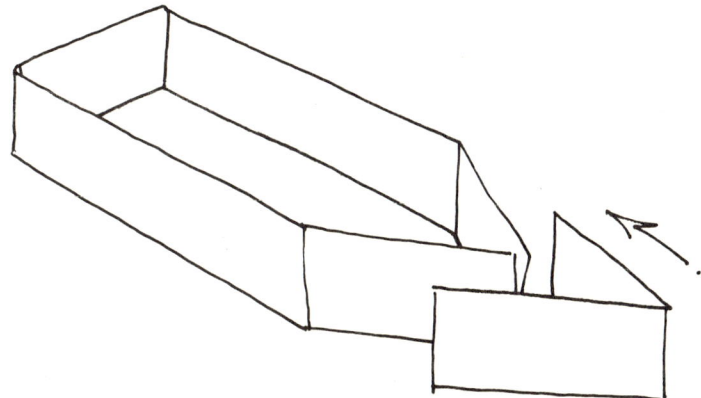

The 4-1/2" × 6" paper is for drawing the seafaring folk who will be captaining these vessels, and the 12-inch square of blue is the water on which they will sail!
Bon voyage!

Lesson 31
Flap-Art

Your kids will love this one! Easy to do and fun to make, this *Flap-Art* greeting card is absolutely *loaded* with surprises!

EACH CHILD WILL NEED:
- drawing paper or pastel-colored construction paper
- pencil and crayons

THE TEACHER WILL NEED:

• a single-edge razor blade or hobby knife, and a desk-protecting sheet of cardboard

TO PRESENT:

1. The drawing paper is folded in half widthwise. Now—with the fold positioned at the top—have your kids draw a picture in which people are seen admiring one or more wall-hung picture frames. (See the figure below for suggestions.) "The pictures," you explain, "will be along later—so just leave the areas inside the picture frames blank for now, and spend your time working on the rest of the drawing."

2. Once your kids are far enough along in their drawings to have established where the hung pictures will go, it will be your job to call them to your desk—one at a time—and perform the following operations.

Using your razor blade and your desk-protecting sheet of cardboard as your working surface, cut the sides of each picture-to-be through *both* thicknesses of the folded paper as indicated here by the heavy lines.

Curtain Raisers 95

Unfold, and cut on the heavy lines.

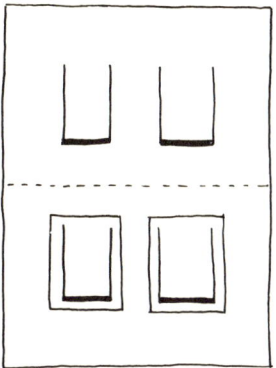

3. Refold. The back flaps are then pushed through the double thickness of the folded paper to cover the front flaps.

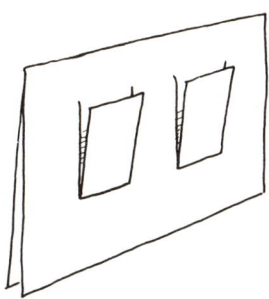

4. The picture frames are now "loaded" and ready to accept whatever art work your young artists care to supply.

5. After the pictures have been crayoned in, invite your kids to open their cards—and *presto*! The art theft of the century will take place under their very noses as the loaded flaps flick the pictures right out of their frames and whisk them away "to a back room"!

6. Now, returning to the picture frames once again, have your kids use this newly acquired space within their picture frames to "load" some kind of a soon-to-be hidden message.

Then reload and *abracadabra*—it "works" every time!

Lesson 32
Paper Roses

Whoever invented this fold must have been an artist of great sensitivity; for *Paper Roses* is paper folding seen at its very best!

To Make the Basic Flower

EACH CHILD WILL NEED:

- 1-1/2" × 18" strips of flower-colored construction paper (red, white, pink, yellow, etc.)

THE TEACHER WILL NEED:

- a stapler (preferably a hand stapler or a stapling pliers*)

TO PRESENT:

1. Beginning from the bottom lefthand corner, roll your strips by hand** until a short stem is formed.

---

* See "Tricks, Shortcuts, Etcetera . . .": For a discussion of staplers, pages 200–201.
** For paper rolling techniques, see *Paper Straws*, method #2, page 198.

Curtain Raisers

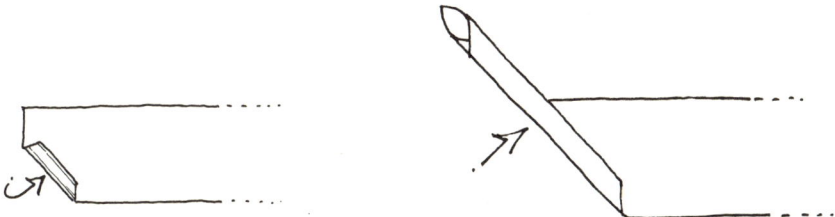

2. Turn upside down, make a right-angle fold, give a slight clockwise twist to the stem, and continue making right-angle folds with the left hand and twisting the stem with the right hand until the flower is completed and secured with a staple.

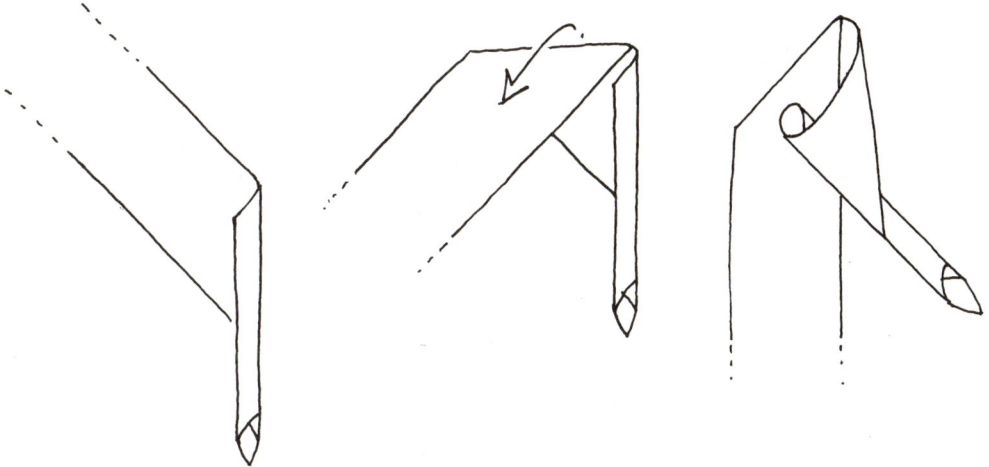

ROSE-MAKING ACTIVITIES

Activity 1: Corsages

EACH CHILD WILL NEED:

- a few completed roses (see instructions above)
- tape
- tissue paper
- ribbon

To Assemble: Simply bind the stems of the roses together, wrap with tissue paper and tie with ribbons.

Activity 2: As Pretty As a Picture

EACH CHILD WILL NEED:

- paper roses
- 12" × 18" drawing paper or pastel-colored construction paper
- pencil, scissors and crayons

THE TEACHER WILL NEED:

- a roll of tape

TO PRESENT:

1. Invite your kids to draw a vase and to add stems as suggested here.

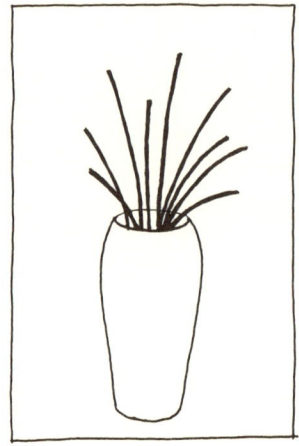

Curtain Raisers

2. At the top of each stem, have your kids use the points of their pencils to puncture a small hole.* Insert a rose into each hole and tape from behind.

Display and admire!

Lesson 33
Link Weaving

Fair warning: *Link Weaving* is not for the very young. Furthermore, it is highly contagious and—once started—may reach epidemic proportions before it can be brought under control.

So don't say that I didn't warn you!

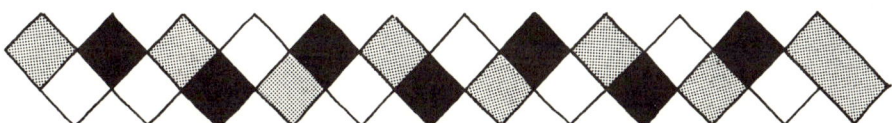

EACH CHILD WILL NEED:
- myriad sheets of 2" × 4-1/2" lightweight paper (*not* construction paper) in various colors**

TO PRESENT:

1. Have your kids fold each link lengthwise, unfold, fold the long sides to the middle, and fold again on the middle fold to make a long narrow packet of paper. Fold this packet in half widthwise, unfold, and fold the short ends to the middle. Fold again on the middle fold and that's that! (See illustrations at top of next page.)

---

* If this hole proves to be too small to receive the stem of the rose, carefully widen the hole with the tapered handle of a classroom paint brush.

** In my experience, a limited color scheme works best: blue and white; red, white, and blue; etc.

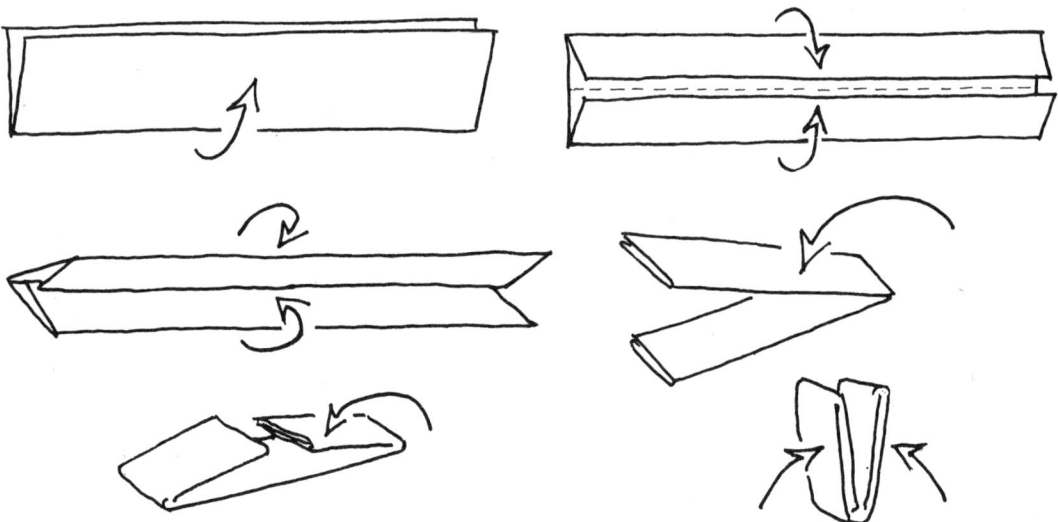

2. Once your kids have learned how to fold the basic units, have them take a closer look at these folded packets as you help them to identify the "good" and the "bad" sides: the "good" side being that which looks like the figure on the left; the bad, as the figure on the right.

3. When your kids are ready to begin to assemble their links, advise them to: (1) pencil an "X" on both sides of the first link, and (2) *always* insert a "bad side up" through a "good side."

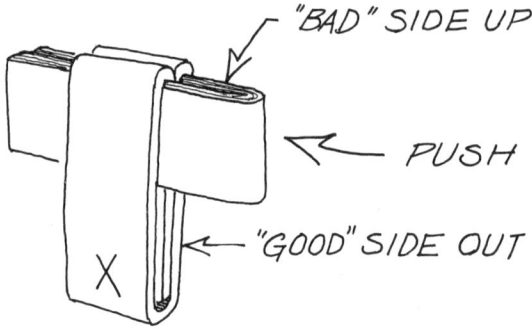

4. After the first two units have been linked, the assembly is then turned upside down to accept the next link.

Curtain Raisers

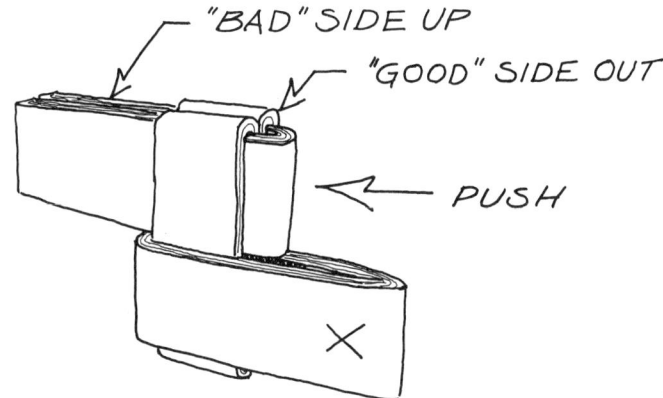

5. From this point on, *your* primary responsibility will simply be to keep enough paper on hand to supply the needs of your class!

Lesson 34
Heads Up!

I've seen many classroom kite projects that, for one reason or another, never got off the ground. Here, on the other hand, is a ready-to-go bit of paper folding that can be aloft within minutes! Educational? You bet! Inexpensive? Couldn't be cheaper! Fun? You bet it's fun! *Heads Up!* is in a class by itself. Don't miss it!

EACH CHILD WILL NEED:

- 8-1/2" square of lightweight paper (typing paper, duplicating, mimeo, copier, etc.)
- a length of thread
- crayons

THE TEACHER WILL NEED:

- a sharp-pointed instrument (a compass point, a large safety pin, etc.)
- rags (preferably sheeting)
- extra thread for those who will forget to bring in their own!

TO PRESENT:

1. Have your kids fold their papers in half diagonally, unfold, *sailboat** each side to the center line, and fold again.

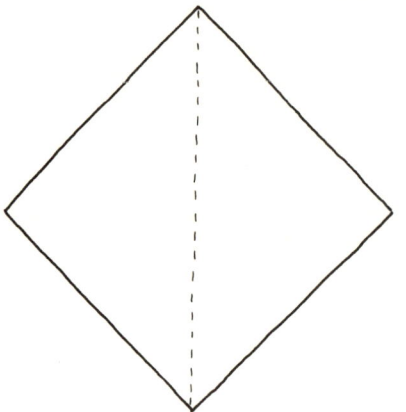 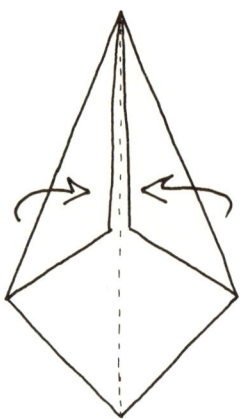 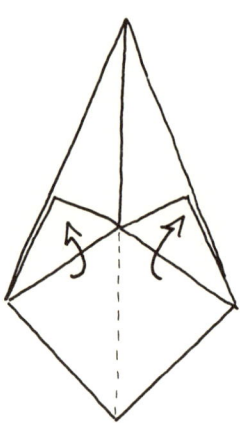

2. The kite is now ready for a few personal touches.

---

* See "Tricks, Shortcuts, Etcetera . . ." (pages 198–199).

Curtain Raisers

3. A small hole is then punched into the forward point of each bridle, the bridle strap is made from a short length of thread, and the end of the remaining thread is tied to the center of the bridle strap.

4. Very narrow strips of lightweight cloth are tied together to make short tails. (Longer tails can be added as needed.) A small puncture hole is made at the base of each kite to receive the tail, and—with that—your classroom fleet will be ready to take to the skies!

Flying Suggestions: A kite this fragile is, of course, a fair-weather craft that will perform best in a very gentle breeze. The stronger the breeze, the longer the tail, so if your kite begins to behave erratically, adjust accordingly!

Lesson 35
From Out of the Shadows...

Shadow shows are always entertaining—but some shows are more entertaining than others. Here is one of the best!

EACH CHILD WILL NEED:

- 5-1/2" × 8-1/2" lightweight white paper (typing, mimeo, duplicating, copier, etc.)
- 8-1/2" × 11" black construction paper plus additional smaller pieces as needed
- a snippet of masking tape
- a shared pattern (see *Preparations*)
- pencils, scissors and crayons

THE TEACHER WILL NEED:

- 5-1/2" × 8-1/2" sheet of tagboard (or other pattern-weight paperboard)
- a single-edge razor blade or hobby knife, and a desk-protecting sheet of cardboard

PREPARATIONS:

Prepare a few tagboard patterns as shown here.

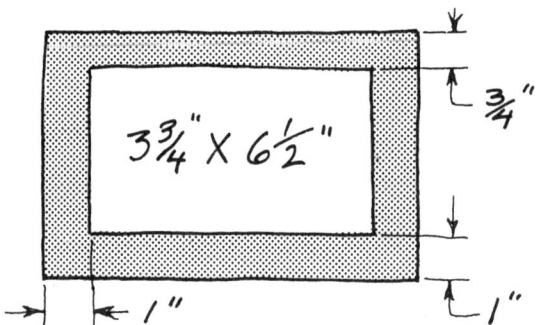

Now that you have come this far, let's see if I can talk you into giving this lesson the best of all possible sendoffs by having you make a shadow theater of your own. Here's how:

1. Fold your 8-1/2" × 11" sheet of black construction paper in half widthwise, unfold, and trace the interior rectangle of cut-out pattern onto the lower half of your black paper.

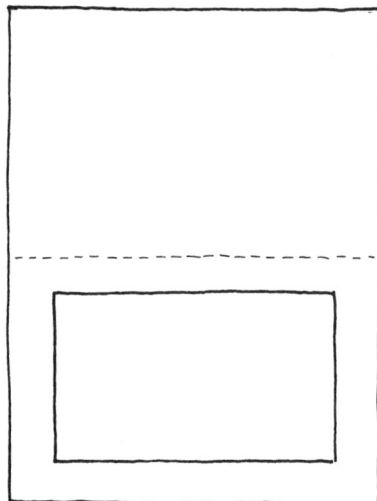

2. When your tracing is complete, refold the black paper and cut out the theater screen through both thicknesses of the black paper.

3. The white papers are then prepared to provide the sets for the coming show. Here are a few good suggestions:

- Just as in the *Salted Eggs* lesson (see pages 82–84), these shadow shows are seen at their best when the stage sets are drawn or applied to the reverse side of the picture screen. (This information will, or course, be crucial if you plan to incorporate lettering into your scenario!)
- While the most effective background sets are made with cut and pasted black paper or drawn with a black crayon, this advice will be largely unheeded by those in your class who will prefer a full-color treatment.
- Make all actors, etc., out of black paper, using close-ups or distance shots—or both—as desired.

- Moonlit (or neonlit) scenes can be made by using two sheets of white paper. The following figure on the left shows how the second sheet is prepared. When this second sheet is placed behind the first, the resulting effect is as shown here at the right.

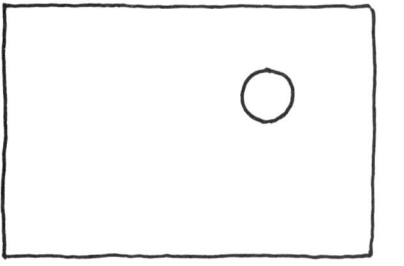 

- And now, here is the part of the lesson that your kids will love most of all. To create a free-flying, black paper, come-and-go bat, ghost, bird, etc., simply attach the flying whatever to the eraser end of your pencil with a snippet of balled-up tape and experiment in front of a lighted window. (This dramatic fade-in and fade-out effect has to be seen to be appreciated!)

TO PRESENT:

Once your kids have prepared their own shadow theaters as explained in Steps 1 and 2, it is time for *your* act to go on. Take your theater and all of your props to the classroom window. Show the screen blank, bring your theater up to the window and—on with the show! (Your plot need not be any more complex than having one of your cut-out performers "walk" across the set muttering something appropriate.)

Curtain Raisers

Then, after you have introduced your kids to the "back-stage" secrets, turn them loose on their own productions.

AND FINALLY:

When the time is ripe, return to the window to show your kids how to give life to a flying creature.

They'll love it!

Lesson 36
Barkin' Dogs

If there are two things that kids love, it is live animals and pictures that *move*; and if, as in *Barkin' Dogs*, you combine these two ideas, then you have a lesson that is *guaranteed* to succeed!

Here's how:

Variation 1: Barkin' and Waggin'

EACH CHILD WILL NEED:

- 9" × 18" drawing paper
- pencil, scissors and crayons

TO PRESENT:

   1. Have your kids fold their drawing paper in half widthwise and then fold in about one and one-half inch on each side.

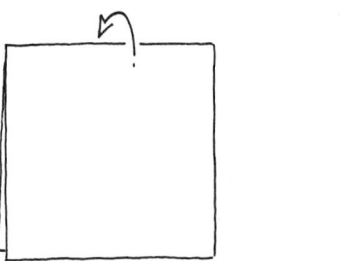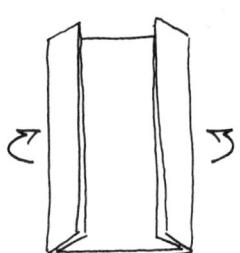

   2. Then explain to your class that you will be calling each child to your desk—one at a time—so that you can make two cuts in each paper: one for a mouth and the other for a tail!

   The paper is then unfolded from the position shown and refolded. The dark lines indicate the nature and the placement of the mouth and tail cuts.

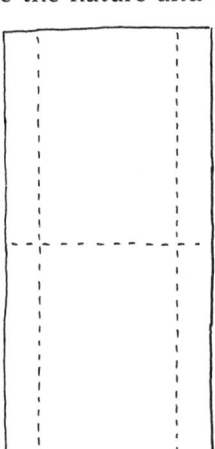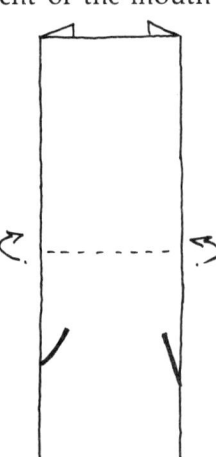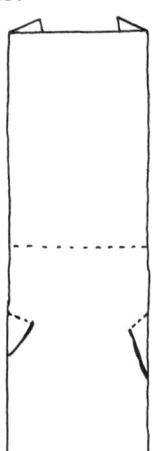

   3. Fold each cut on the diagonal and then fold back and forth on this same fold a couple of times to help it lose its "memory."

   4. The paper is then returned to the Step 1 position, where the nose and the tail are then popped out.

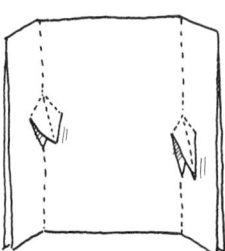

Curtain Raisers   109

5. And once your kids see the willingness with which each dog will "bark" and wag its tail, your job is just to get out of the way and let your kids get to work!

Variation 2: The Reception Committee

EACH CHILD WILL NEED:

- 9" × 12" drawing paper
- pencils, scissors and crayons

TO PRESENT:

1. Have your kids fold their drawing papers in half widthwise, unfold, and then fold in half lengthwise. Now fold each end in to touch the center fold.

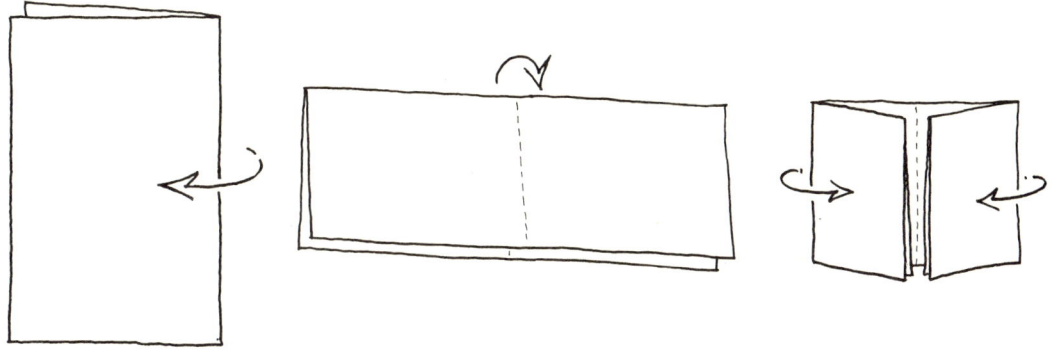

2. Unfold these last two (side) folds, and then turn the paper over to make a new fold. Now make the very same folds on the right hand side of the paper.

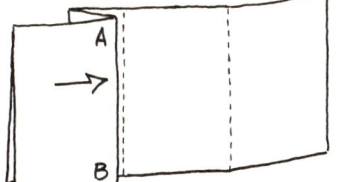 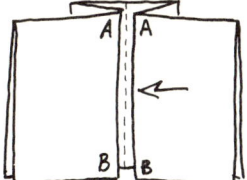

3. Unfold all folds. Fold in the sides and cut on the heavy lines. Fold each cut on the diagonal, and exercise these folds before returning the paper to the position shown below at the far right.

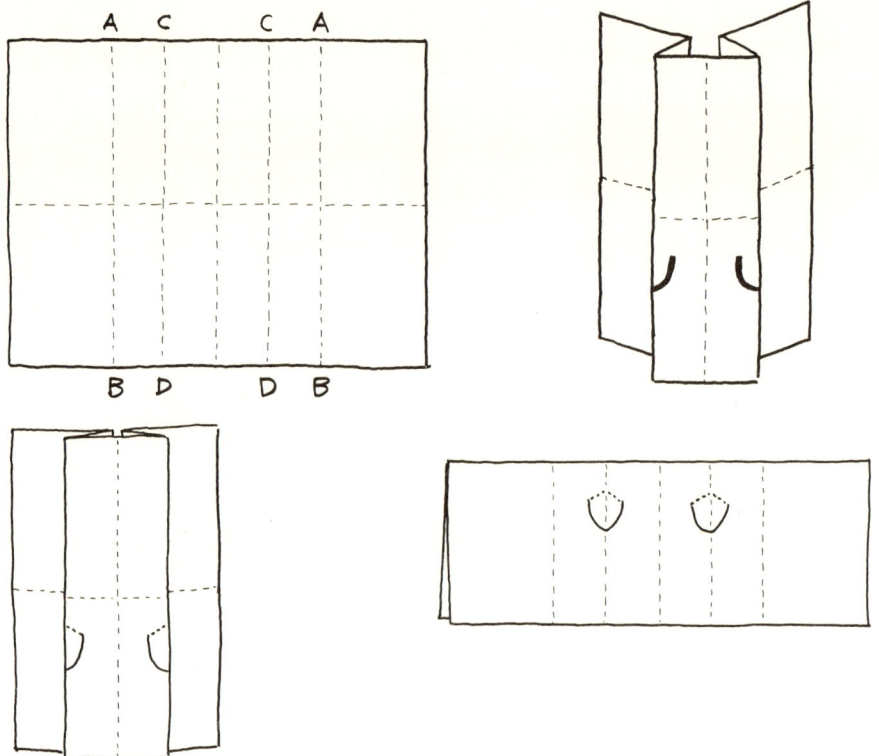

4. Pop out the muzzles and let your kids go to work!

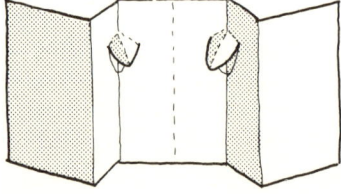

Lesson 37
Jumpin' Frogs

Not only can this frog jump, but it has a voice that you won't believe! And for a recreational art project—who could ask for anything more?

EACH CHILD WILL NEED:

- 9" × 12" green construction paper

Curtain Raisers   111

- 8-1/2" square of lightweight white paper (typing, duplicating, mimeo, copier, etc.)
- a shared 3-1/2" (watercup size) circle pattern
- a three foot (+ or −) length of thread
- two short scraps of tape
- paste, pencils, scissors and crayons

THE TEACHER MAY NEED:

- a stapler

TO PRESENT:

1. Have your kids position their circle pattern onto their green paper and trace lightly with a pencil. This traced circle is then used as the starting point for drawing a "pear," and then transforming it into a big fat frog. Cut out the frog, place a dot in the center of the traced circle and then cut on the heavy line.

 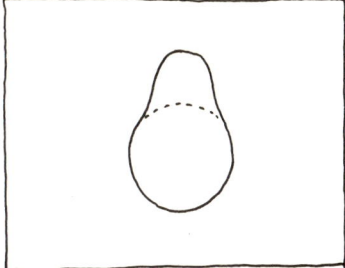

 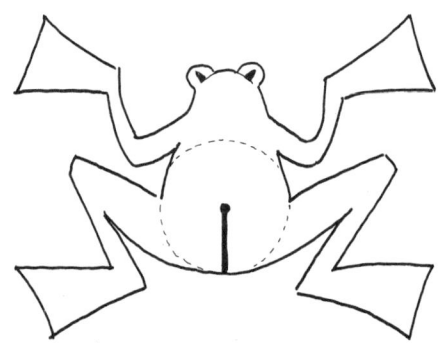

2. The 8-1/2-inch square is rolled into a paper straw using one or another of the methods shown in "Tricks, Shortcuts and Etcetera . . .," pages 197–198. Secure the completed straw with a scrap of tape.

3. Like all windpipe operations, this next part is a little tricky—but it is well worth the effort:

The first figure below represents one end of the paper straw. Starting from point A, two small surgical snips are made to each side of the windpipe to create the triangular flap in the middle figure. Carefully bend this flap down as shown in the third figure.

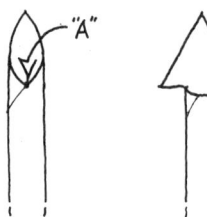 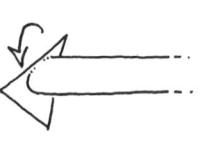

To make the frog croak, hold the uncut end of the windpipe to your lips and gently suck in. If the suction is either two strong or too slight, the flap will not vibrate; so, reserve plenty of time for a high-spirited practice session.

Curtain Raisers

AND FINALLY:

Once the sound of croaking frogs begin to fill the room, have your kids tape one end of their thread to the underbelly of the frog. The frog is then *circleconed** and pasted or stapled. The other end of the thread is tied to the shank of the frog's windpipe so that the creature can both jump and croak at the same time!

Lesson 38
And Flyin' Fish

If it has been a long, hard week, and it's time to let off a little steam—what you need is a room full of *Flyin' Fish*!

EACH CHILD WILL NEED:

- construction paper in assorted colors:
    - 3" × 4-1/2"
    - 2" × 9"
    - 6" × 9"
- 1-1/2" × 4-1/2" white paper (two each)
- paste, pencils, scissors and crayons
- possibly a rubber band or two

THE TEACHER WILL NEED:

- a single-edge razor blade or hobby knife, and a desk-protecting sheet of cardboard
- a small stapler or, preferably, a *stapling pliers***

---

* See "Tricks, Shortcuts, Etcetera. . ." page 192.

** For a discussion of these and other varieties of classroom staplers see "Tricks, Shortcuts, Etcetera . . .", pages 191–200.

PREPARATIONS:

Cut a three-inch horizontal slit into each of the 6" × 9" sheets of colored paper, and two smaller diagonal slits.

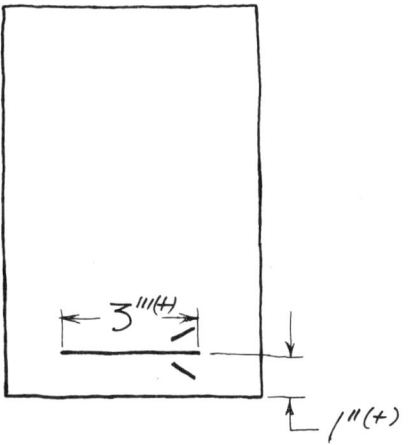

TO PRESENT:

1. From one of the small pieces of white paper, have your kids draw, cut out, and paste a couple of fish eyes, and add a few U-shaped fish scales to the 6" × 9" paper.

2. The 3" × 4-1/2" construction paper is then cut in half widthwise. One of these halves can be turned into a fin by folding. Then insert the top part of this fin through the slot of the larger paper and secure to the underside of body paper with paste. The 2-1/4" × 3" remainder is then cut into fin-like pieces and pasted into the diagonal slits.

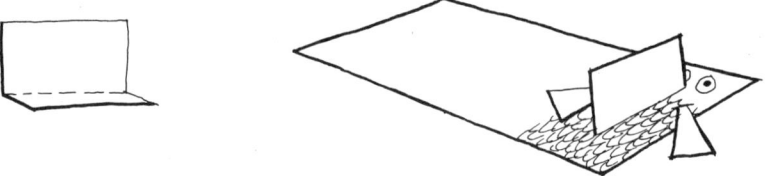

3. And while your kids are hard at work on the body of the fish, it is your job to staple the 2" × 9" tailpiece.

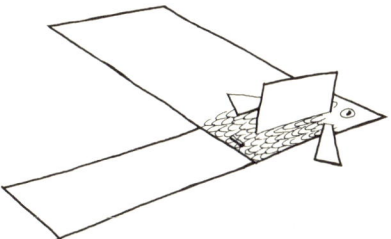

4. The tailpieces are then fringed lengthwise. And the remaining piece of white paper is cut to make teeth (and continued in Step 6).

5. The rest is easy. The paper is turned upside down and rolled up to form a cylindrical fish. The body is then either pasted or stapled or, if necessary, simply secured with a couple of rubber bands.

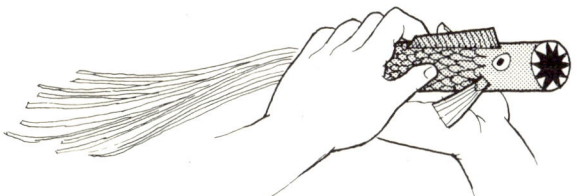

6. And the teeth? The teeth are rolled up and inserted like dentures! These teeth can either stick out or be turned inward.

FLYING INSTRUCTIONS:

The Illusion: With mischievous grins, the children carry their fish home to show their parents. "You can pet my fish if you want to," says the child, but the moment the parents reach out to do so, the fish *leaps* out of the child's hands and sails halfway across the room!

The Secret: The fish is held with the tensed (but hidden) middle finger of the supporting hand resting on the underside back tip of the fish's body—just waiting for the *right* moment to spring the trap

The parent's hand reaches out, the fish gets nervous, the hidden finger snaps forward and—EEK!—the startled parent recoils "in fright" as the *Flyin' Fish* leaps into the air with the speed of an angry marlin!

Beware!

3
Magical Improvizations

Your kids have completed all their regular assignments, and you're finding yourself way ahead of schedule. But since it's too late to begin another unit and too early to dismiss your class, what do you do until the bell rings?

Check one:

- Hem and haw?
- Allow chaos to reign?
- Or do you reach into your well-worn bag of tricks and try to come up with a good, rousing crowd-pleaser?

If you have checked off applause-winning answer 3, then I suggest that you get ready for a standing ovation!

Each of the following lessons has been designed so that it can either be presented separately or linked together with other lessons to make presentations of almost any length. Furthermore, once you have had an opportunity to look these lessons over, I think you will agree with me that this chapter contains some of the best short material that has ever been gathered together in one place—and that it is the chance discovery of lessons like these that continue to make teaching *fun*!

Lesson 1
The Origami Cup

If your kids are like my kids, the thought of turning a piece of paper into a drinking utensil will be enough to send cheerful shivers of anticipation from one end of the classroom to the other!

So if your kids don't already know how to make an origami cup—it's time they learned!

EACH CHILD WILL NEED:

- a sheet of paper (typing, duplicating, mimeo, copier, etc.)
- probably a pair of scissors (see Step 1)

TO PRESENT:

1. The Origami Cup begins with a square sheet of paper. If your paper is already square, fold it once diagonally and move on to Step 2.

If your paper is rectangular, begin with the sailboat fold* and cut off the "boat."

2. After briefly explaining to your kids the meaning of the word *parallel*, use a work-along demonstration piece to take your class through the following set of instructions:

With the folded paper positioned as shown, fuss with corner A until A-B becomes parallel to C-D.

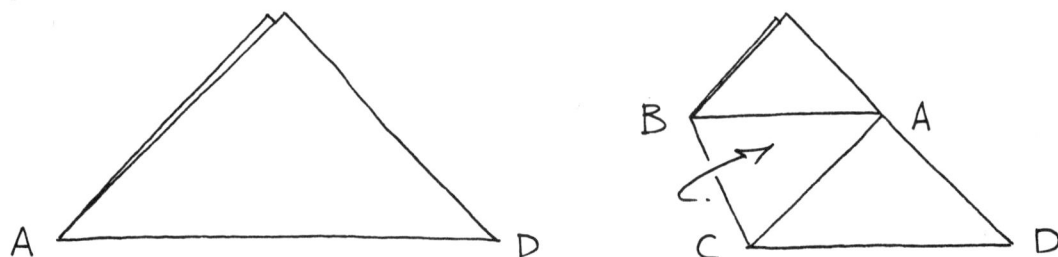

3. Now that the hard part is done, the rest is easy! Fold up corner D to point B, turn down the two top flaps, and the cup is now complete!

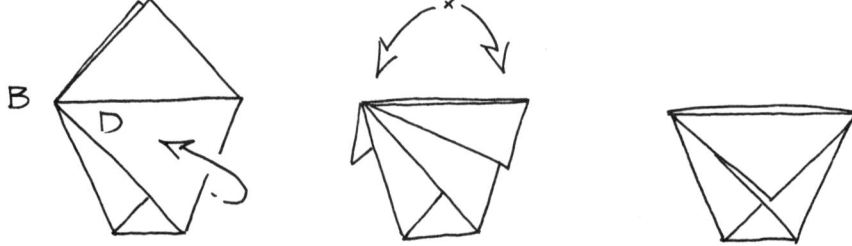

- You can drink out of it, you can even boil water in it.
- Or make it from a sheet of newspaper and you have a "cup" large enough to be worn as a hat!
- Or—if you don't need a hat, use it as a mailbox.

---

* See "Tricks, Shortcuts, Etcetera. . ." under *Sailboating* (page 198).

Magical Improvizations

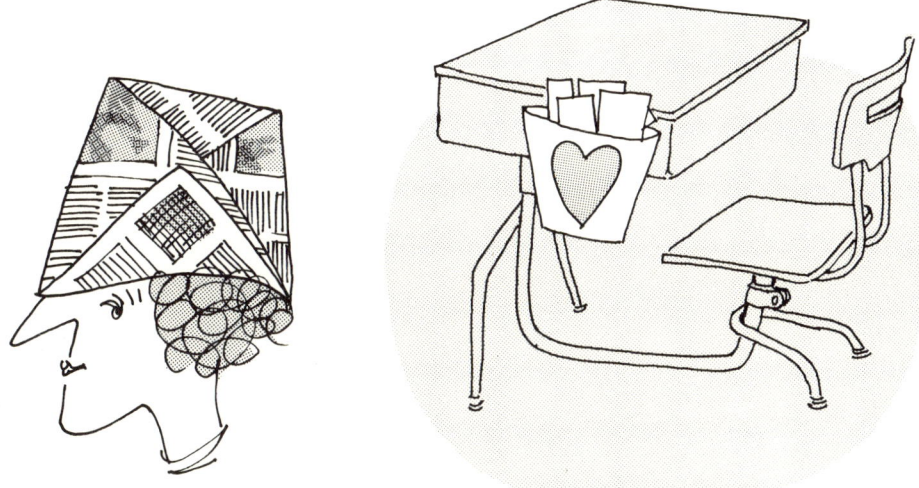

And if you would like to see still another way to put this cup to good use, be sure to see the *Blabbermouths* that are waiting to greet you on page 27.

Lesson 2
The Flexasquare

Of all the origami creations known to children, none have ever surpassed the popularity of the *Flexasquare*. Passed on like a skip rope song from one generation of children to the next, this traditional paper fold is better known to kids as the "Fortune Teller," the "Cootie Catcher," or sometimes even as the "Candy Dish Fold." But what about your kids? Can *they* do it?

EACH CHILD WILL NEED:

- a sheet of lightweight paper (typing, duplicating, mimeo, copier, etc.)
- scissors

TO PRESENT:

1. Using the sailboat fold (see page 198), cut off the "boat" and save the "sail."
2. Then add the following folds.

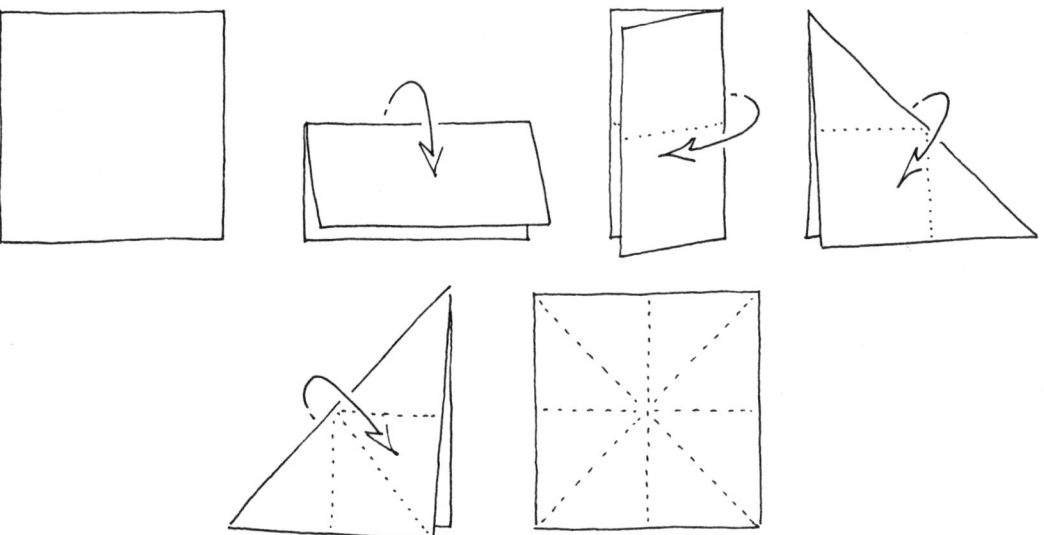

3. Once this paper has been prefolded as shown, it is time to begin the concluding series of folds.

Following the example below, fold all corners to the center of the paper. And then turn the folded paper over.

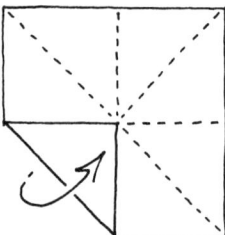 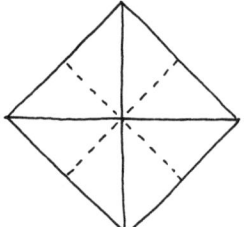 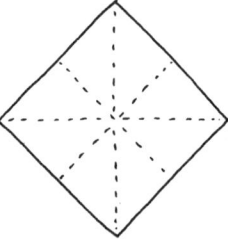

Fold the new corners to the center of the paper as begun in the first figure and completed in the second figure. Then turn the folded paper over so that the side with the four square flaps is uppermost.

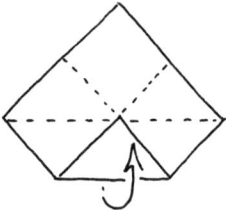 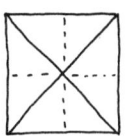 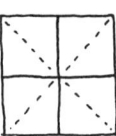

4. Even before you have had a chance to complete your own work-along flexa-square, you'll look up to find that some of your kids will already be one step ahead

Magical Improvizations

of you. But while some will have opened their flexasquares with the ease of a Japanese origami master, there will be others in your classroom who will need your help!

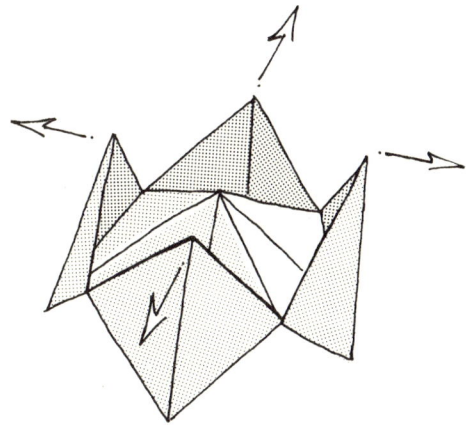

To many children, the completion of a "working" flexasquare is an accomplishment that engenders more wonder than does the most sophisticated piece of electronic hardware. Your kids didn't buy the flexasquare, they didn't assemble it from prefabricated parts—they made it *themselves*, and they did so from nothing more complicated than a simple square of paper!

Some of the girls in your class will already possess arcane formulas for using this creation as a Fortune Teller. (You won't have to *ask* them "how to do it"—they'll *tell* you!)

And here are some other great follow-up ideas:

The Candy Dish

The obliging flexasquare makes a very servicable candy dish. Just open and fill!

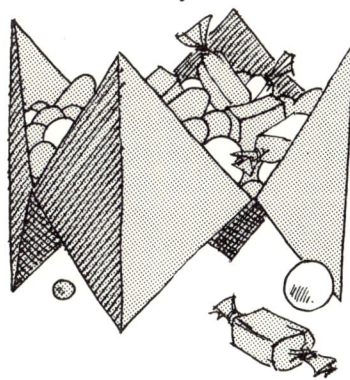

The Cootie Catcher

Since the word "cootie" is World War I slang for a body louse, the popular Cootie Catcher has to be at least as old as its name.

1. Hold the finished flexasquare in your hand. There are, as you can see, four digital pockets that can accomodate your thumb and three fingers, and eight triangular facets on the inside of the display face that can be alternately opened and closed to present two totally different sets of interior views.

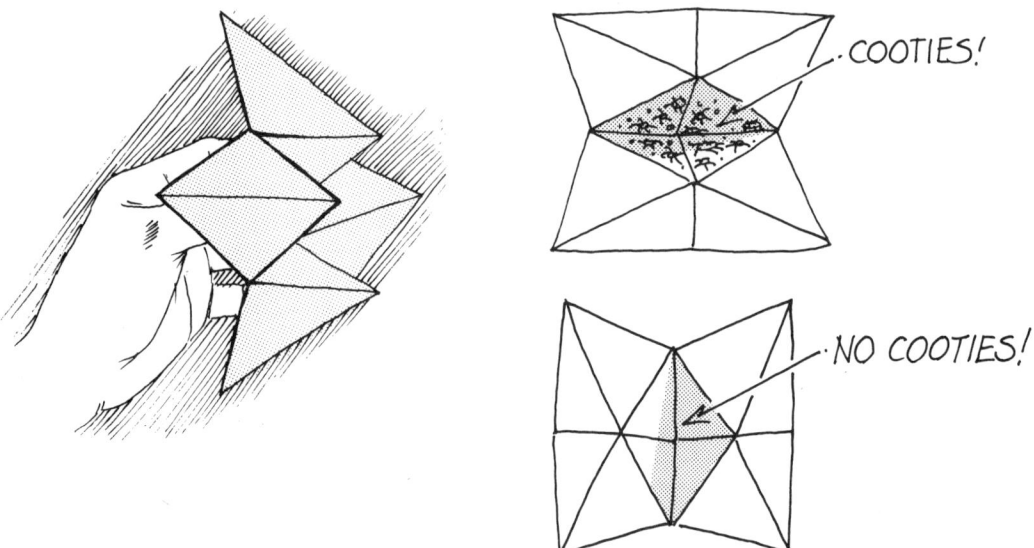

2. Now if one of those interiors is peppered with penciled or crayoned "cooties" and then withdrawn from view, the alternate interior can be shown to be "clean." The prankster then makes a grab at somebody's sleeve and then closes the "catcher."

When opened (to reveal the hidden pocket)—*presto!* A whole nest of "cooties" have mysteriously appeared from nowhere!

Solemnly shaking the "catcher" to dispose of the cooties, the cootie hunter again shows the interior clean before gleefully stalking off to find another victim!

Another Good Use for the Flexasquare: The flexasquare can also be used to make a wonderful flying creature with restlessly snapping jaws; so be sure to investigate the colony of *Attack-Bats* that live on page 34.

Lesson 3
A Couple of Real Bangers

I don't know whether the children of Ancient Egypt folded their papyri into *Bangers*, but these paper toys have been around for a long time!

Here's how:

Activity 1: Primary Bangers

EACH CHILD WILL NEED:

- a square of lightweight paper* (typing paper, duplicating, mimeo, copier, etc.)

---

* Or have your kids make their own *Sailboat Squares*. (See "Tricks, Shortcuts, Etcetera. . .", page 198.)

TO PRESENT:

1. Have your kids fold their squares on the diagonal and then repeatedly reverse these folds until they begin to lose their memory.

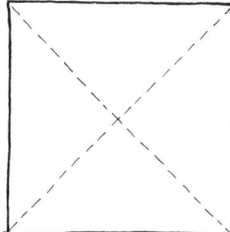

2. Unfold and fold in half.

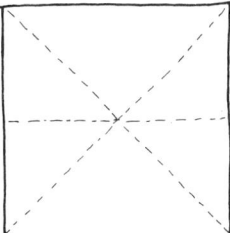

3. Press in the folded ends (see arrows) until both flaps are hidden from view.

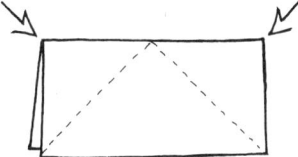 

To Operate: Simply hold, as shown below, and bring your arm down sharply.

BANG!

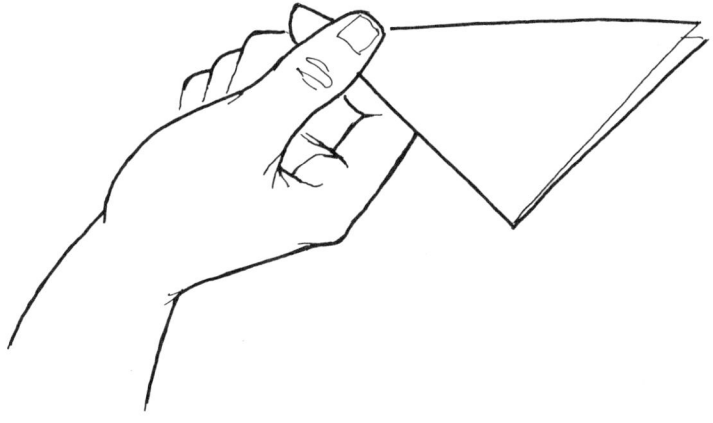

Activity 2: Heavy Duty Bangers

EACH CHILD WILL NEED:

- a sheet of 8-1/2" × 11" lightweight paper (typing paper, duplicating, mimeo, copier, etc.)

TO PRESENT:

1. Have your kids fold their papers lengthwise, unfold, and then *sailboat** all four corners.

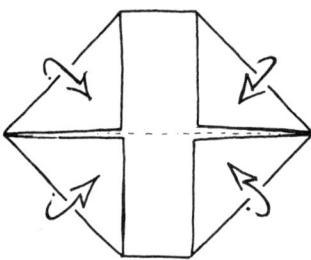

2. Fold in half again, but this time with the flaps inside.

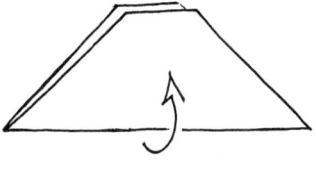

3. Fold.

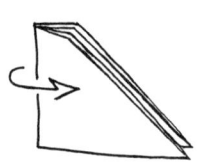 

4. Fold the two sharp corners back, one on each side of the main body of the packet as shown here.

To Operate: Hold the folded paper as shown, bring down sharply and . . . B A N G !

* See "Tricks, Shortcuts, Etcetera. . ." under *Sailboating* (page 198).

Magical Improvizations

Lesson 4
Flying in the Wright Tradition

If space is the last frontier, then the pioneers of tomorrow are the kids who share your classroom. Here are a few top-flight ideas that will go a long way towards keeping that dream aloft!

Aeronautical Idea 1: The Flying "O"

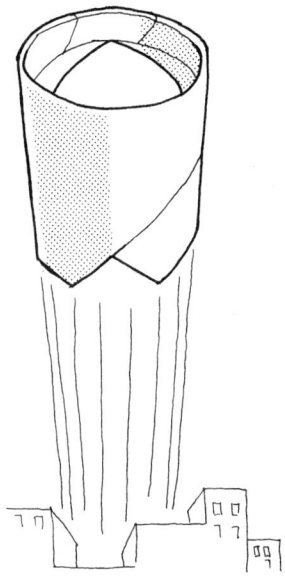

EACH CHILD WILL NEED:

- 8-1/2" × 11" lightweight paper (typing, duplicating, mimeo, copier, etc.)
- a small piece of tape

TO PRESENT:

1. Have your kids fold their paper swallowtail fashion.

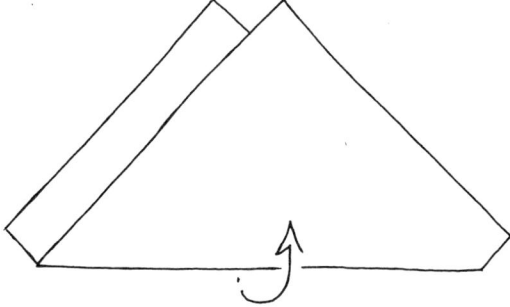

2. Add a series of approximately three folds.

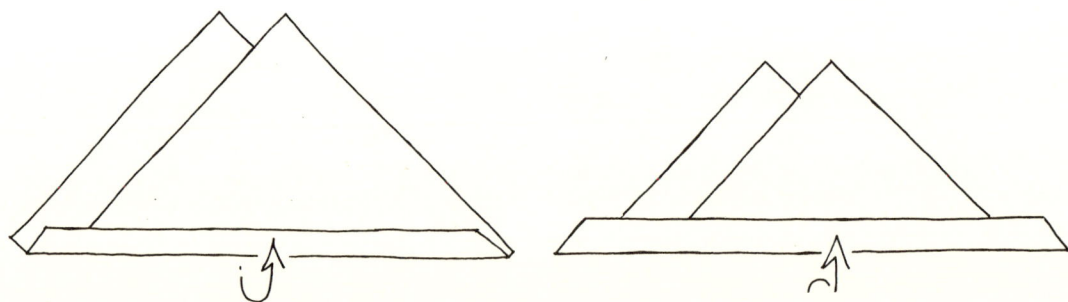

3. Insert one of the folded ends into the other, as shown, and tape to secure.

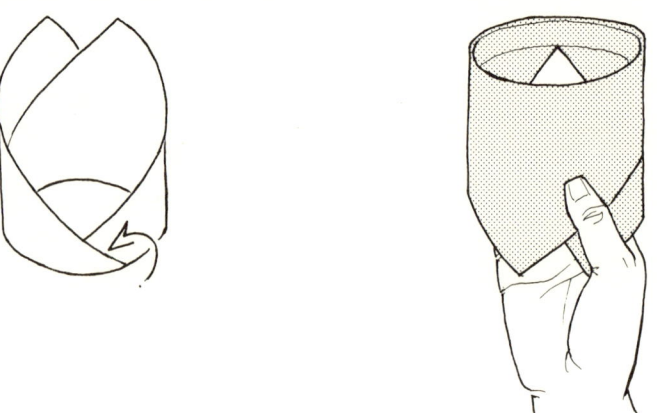

Launching Instructions: Hold the *Flying "O"* swallowtail-down and throw overhand.

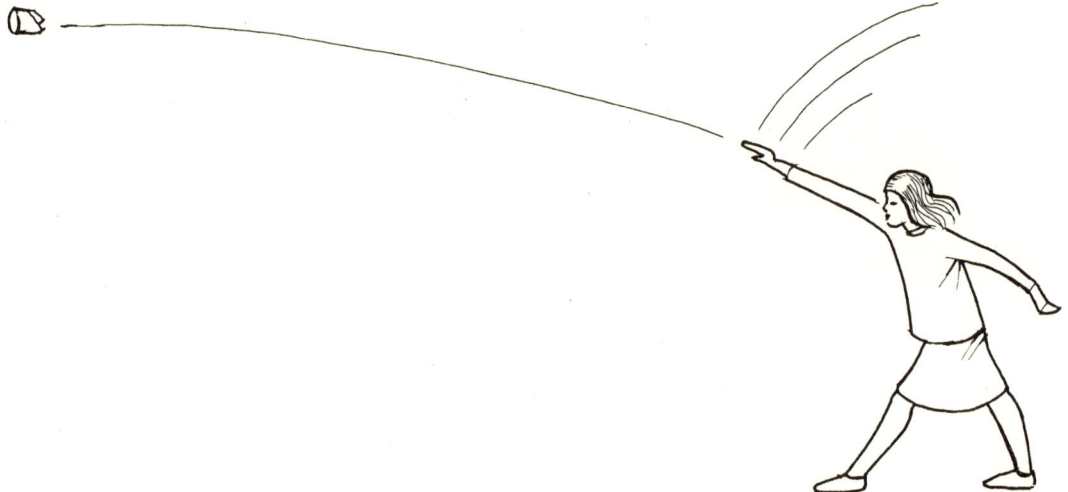

Aeronautical Idea 2: The Last Straw

EACH CHILD WILL NEED:

- 8-1/2" × 11" and 2-1/8" × 11" (+ or −) lightweight paper (typing paper, duplicating, mimeo, copier, etc.)
- a short piece of tape

TO PRESENT:

1. Have your kids roll their 8-1/2" × 11" paper into a *paper straw* using straw-making technique 1 (see Tricks, Shortcuts, Etcetera. . .). Secure with a scrap of tape.
2. The other piece of paper is then cut into strips to make one large and one small loop which are attached gun-sight style to the rolled paper as shown here.

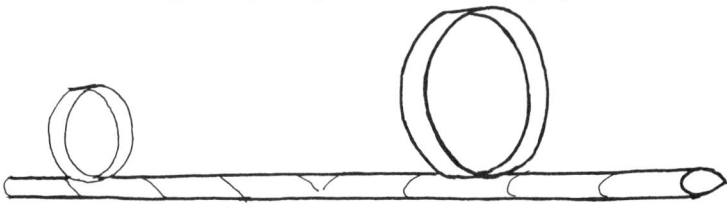

To Launch: Simply throw overhand as you might throw a dart!

Aeronautical Idea 3: The Intercontinental

EACH CHILD WILL NEED:

- a double sheet of newspaper
- long strips of drawing or construction paper
- tape

TO PRESENT:

The *Intercontinental* is really nothing more than a king-size version of the *Last Straw*, but the increase in size adds a proportionate increase in its range.

The Flight of the *Intercontinental* must be seen to be believed!

To Launch: Just hold it like a spear and throw it with as much heft as you can manage!

Aeronautical Idea 4: Rocket-Powered Space Shuttle

EACH CHILD WILL NEED:

- 8-1/2" × 11" lightweight paper (typing, duplicating, mimeo, copier, etc.)
- scissors
- rubber band
- a short stick (an unsharpened pencil, a throat stick, popsicle stick, etc.)

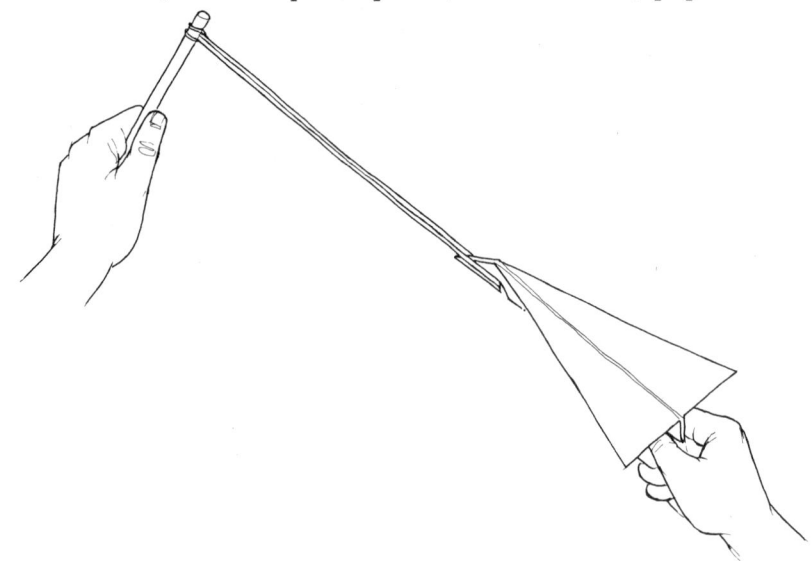

TO PRESENT:

1. Any delta-wing airplane will do, but for those who need help constructing a simple airplane of this sort, these figures should be self-explanatory.

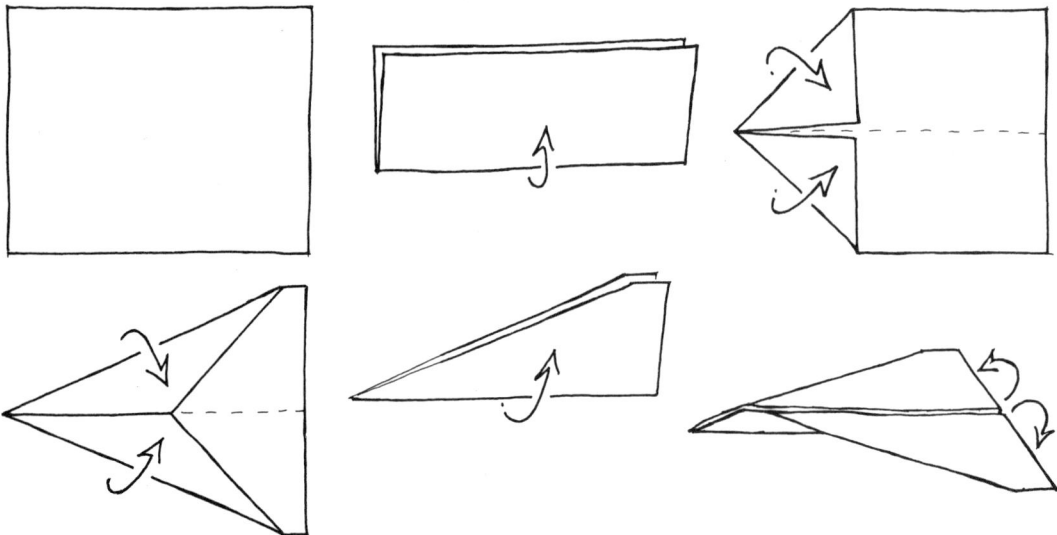

Magical Improvizations   129

   2. When the airplanes are completed, have your kids cut a small notch in the fuselage as suggested here.

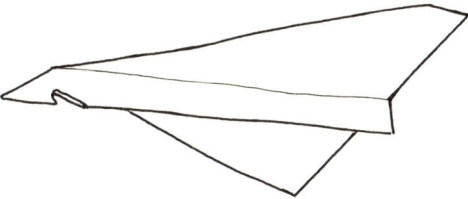

   3. Attach the rubber band to the launching stick.

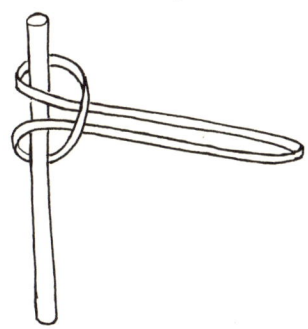

   To Launch: Simply attach the rubber band to the notch, pull back and release! For maximum flight distance, use the launcher as a throwing stick and "follow through" with the swing of your arm.

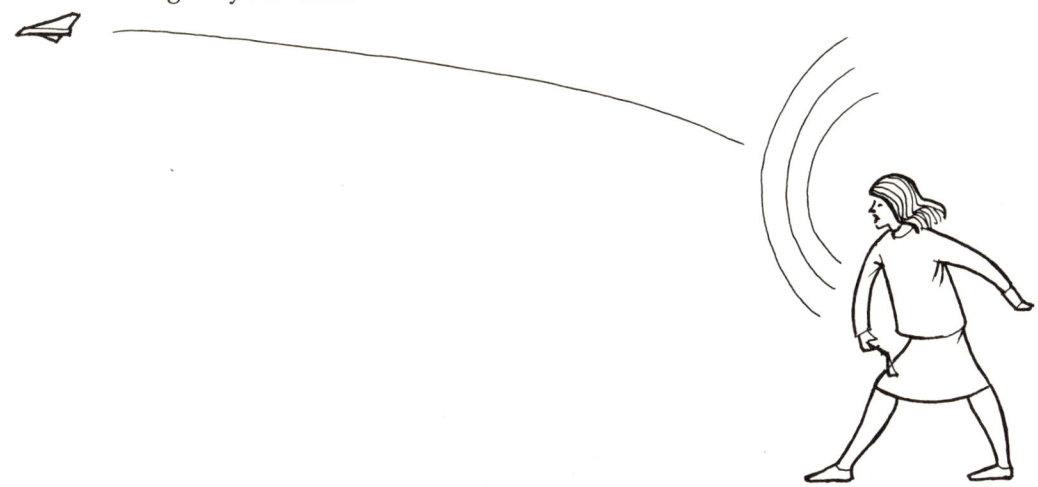

   Other Top-Flight Aeronautical Ideas: See *Heads Up*, the stickless kite lesson that begins on page 101.

AND FINALLY:

   If you can get your hands on my first Parker book (*Paste, Pencils, Scissors and Crayons*, Parker Publishing Co., 1979), don't miss the lesson entitled "My Favorite Airplane"!

Lesson 5
Score Keepers

Five minutes or fifty minutes, here is a paper-based activity flexible enough to fit in anywhere!

EACH CHILD WILL NEED:

- Construction paper in whatever colors and sizes that you have on hand. (And since size is *not* important, this might be the perfect opportunity to use up some of your smaller scraps.)
- pencil and scissors

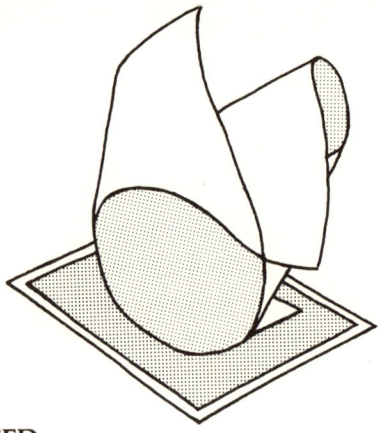

THE TEACHER WILL NEED:

- a stapler
- and probably a roll or two of tape

TO PRESENT:

1. Explain to your class what *scoring* is all about (see page 200 of "Tricks, Shortcuts, Etcetera . . . "), and then just let your kids experiment on their own. See the following figures for some worthwhile suggestions.*

 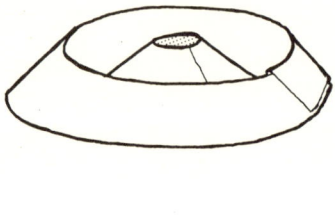

---

* Take a second look at the figure at the top right of page 131 and the figure that began this lesson and tell me what you see. Once you sense that both illustrations were drawn from the same scored sculpture, you can begin to appreciate the wild variety of visual surprises that lie in store for you!

Magical Improvizations   131

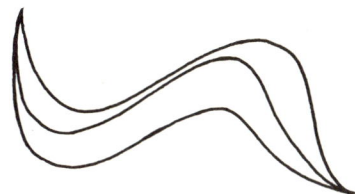 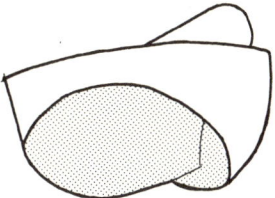

2. The stapler and the tape is for helping your kids to assemble some of their more elaborate creations or to mount their more spectacular pieces on a paper pedestal.

Lesson 6
Mr. Möbius and Mr. Baer

Who is Mr. Möbius? August Ferdinand Möbius (1790–1868) was a famous mathematician and the inventor of the *Möbius Strip*. Mr. Baer, on the other hand, is the not-so-illustrious author of this book and one who would go to any extremes to link his name with greatness:

The Möbius Strip

Boldly stated, the *Möbius Strip* is nothing more than a loop containing a half twist. In other words, the moment that you take a pencil and letter an "A" at one end of a strip of paper and a "B" at the other and then paste *face* "A" to *face* "B," you are ready to begin!

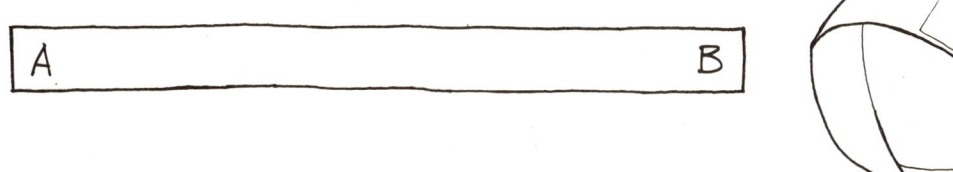

Activity 1: Drawing the Impossible Conclusion

Everybody knows the difference between *inside* and *outside*. Or, as you explain it to your kids, a convict may be able to draw a line around the *inside* of his prison wall but *not* on the *outside*. "For this reason," you say to your class, "as long as I keep drawing a crayon line down the middle of the outside of this paper loop, there is no possible way for me to ever be accused of drawing a line on the *inside*!"

And yet—the moment that your crayon line completes its journey around the "outside" of the Mobius Strip and returns to the point of its origin—it is perfectly obvious to all that the crayon line has indeed traveled around "both" sides of the same strip!

To cries of "But the loop is twisted!," you counter with, "Then does that mean a twisted loop has only one side? How could anything have but one side? That's impossible!"

Activity 2: One Divided by Two Is...?

Taking the same Möbius Strip that you have just finished with in the previous activity, you wonder aloud as to what would happen if you were to cut this strip "down the center line."

"Anybody have any opinions?" you ask.

Your kids will, of course, be happy to volunteer the obvious answer: "You will have *two* twisted loops!"

You cut down the center line and—presto!—instead of two small loops you now have one *large* loop.

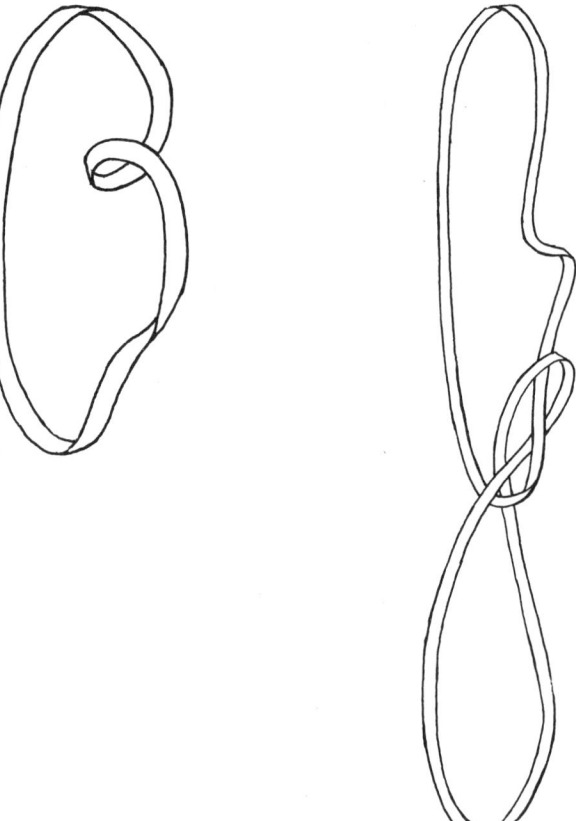

"All right, then," you say to your class, "what do you suppose will happen if I were to cut *this* loop in half down the middle?"

"You'll have one giant twisted loop?"

Again, you cut down the center of the loop, but this time you end up not with a larger loop but with two loops linked together!

I don't know of another three-dimensional paradox that lends itself so readily to further experimentation. Here are two more Möbius creations that you and your kids will enjoy:

Activity 3: Traveling in the Breakdown Lane

In *Activity 1*, when we drew the crayon line down the middle of the Möbius Strip, we found that the two lines eventually met, but not before the crayon had drawn a *center* line on both "sides" of the strip.

This brings us to the next question: what would happen if—instead of drawing a center line for the entire distance—we drew a line just a third of the way in?

Try it and you'll see! The crayon line will eventually return to its starting place, but at no time does this *off*-center line ever travel a route that is directly above or below itself.

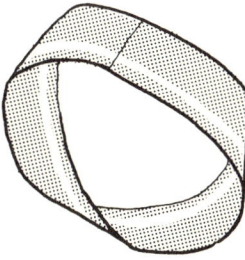

Activity 4: One Divided by Three Is . . . ?

Continuing with this same loop, what would happen if we were to cut on this off-center line?

Oddly enough, the result will be one *large* band linked to one small band, but both of these bands will be the same width!

And which part of the first band went where? ("You'll have to try it again and color in the 'breakdown lane' with crayon to see for yourself what is happening here in Möbius Land!")

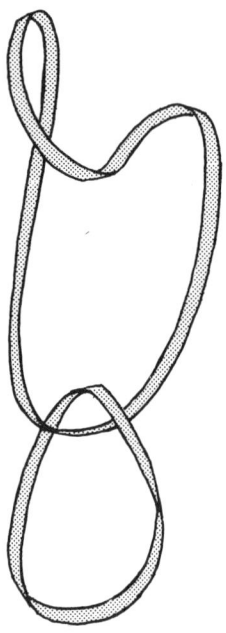

And Mr. Baer?

Born much too late to invent the Möbius Strip, Mr. Baer's only major contribution to the subject of recreational topography has been the *Baer Box*. While Martin Gardner (who is nearly as famous as Mr. Möbius) insists upon calling this invention "a nice variation of the hypercard paradox," the Baer Box is essentially nothing more than a Möbius strip folded into a four-sided box and hinged with a hypercard lid. In other words, if a Möbius Strip can be defined as having neither an inside or an outside, then the Baer Box—which is built upon the same principle—is, by definition, a box for storing all those things that one has no intentions of keeping.

Here are the dimensions. Draw the meandering line, cut on the heavy line, and fold on the dotted lines.

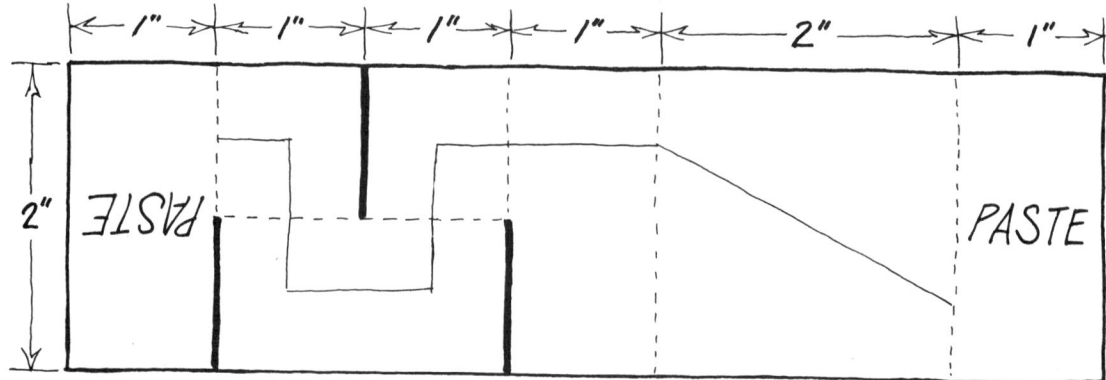

The next figure shows the route for the meandering line as seen on the reverse side of this same strip.

Magical Improvizations

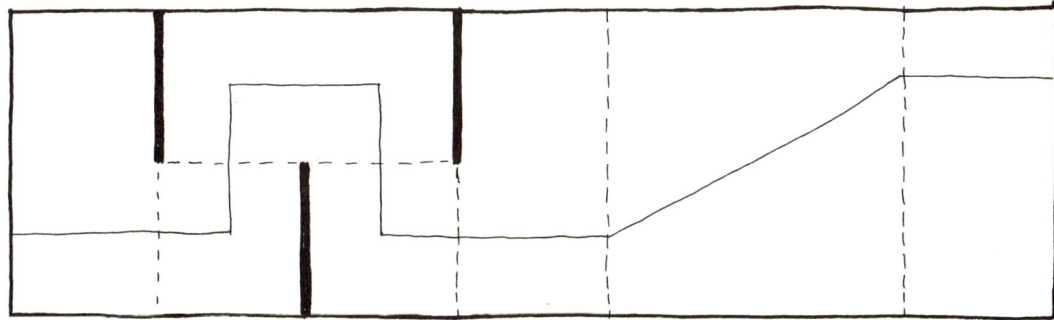

Assemble and paste.

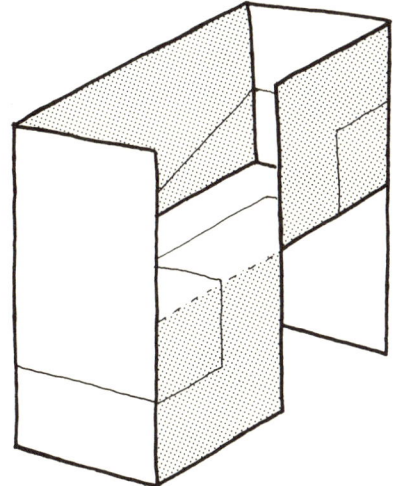

There! By following the meandering line and manipulating the lid, it is possible to "prove" that, like all Möbius creations, this box has neither inside or outside.

Furthermore, if you were to cut on this meandering line, you would end up with one *large* band of paper. Now—just as in Activity 1—cut the resulting strip in half lengthwise and . . . ?

Lesson 7
Squaring the Circle

It's too late in the period to start anything new, but it is also too early to call it quits; so what do you do with your kids in the minutes remaining?

Here is a five-minute lesson that is the best of its kind that I have ever seen. Try it!

THE TEACHER WILL NEED:
- two strips of paper
- scissors and tape

TO PRESENT:

You begin by holding up two strips of paper. "Now watch this very closely," you say with an air of mystery, "because I am going to do something that is going to turn your head inside out."

Making each strip into a loop, you then tape the two loops together.

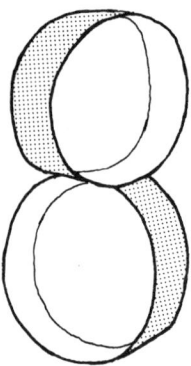

"What do I have now?" you ask as you hold up your double loops for observation. "I have two loops taped together, nothing more and nothing less. Now, what do you think would happen if I were to cut each of these loops in half lengthwise?"

"Four SMALL circles?"

"One BIG circle?"

After these and other speculations have been aired, you cut on the first loop to produce the first surprise.

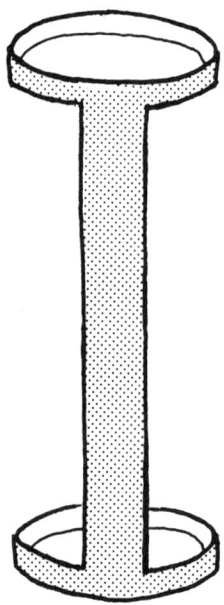

Magical Improvizations

And then, once your kids have recovered from this initial jolt to their expectations, you cut down the center of the second "loop" (which is now the broad connecting strip that joins the two halves of the first loop) to "square the circle."

Lesson 8
Alive and Moving!

Like the portrait in Oscar Wilde's *Picture of Dorian Gray*, each of our *Alive and Moving!* pictures are about to take on a life of their own. Read on and you'll see what I mean!

EACH CHILD WILL NEED:

- 8-1/2" × 11" lightweight white paper (typing paper, duplicating, mimeo, copier, etc.)
- black construction paper
- pencil and scissors

THE TEACHER WILL NEED:

- a large stapler
- some kind of bright, portable light (either battery-powered or otherwise). My favorite light for this purpose is a high-powered lightbulb housed in a hemispherical reflector but, with a little experimentation on your part, I am sure that you will find something just as suitable!

TO PRESENT:

1. Invite your kids to use their black paper to draw a silhouette of a snake rising out of a basket. (The cut-out snake and basket might look something like that pictured here.)

2. Staple the head of the snake and staple the basket, but do so in such a way so that the body of the snake is raised from the surface of the white paper.

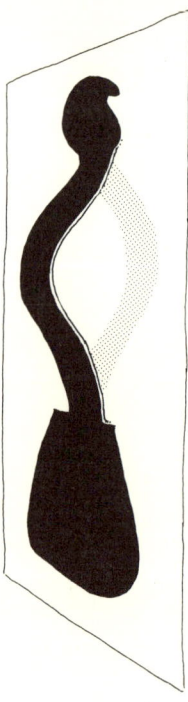

3. Then turn off the classroom lights, hum a little Eastern music in a minor key, and—one snake at a time—bring these creatures to life by turning your snake's back to the audience and by moving your light in a slow, rhythmic motion!

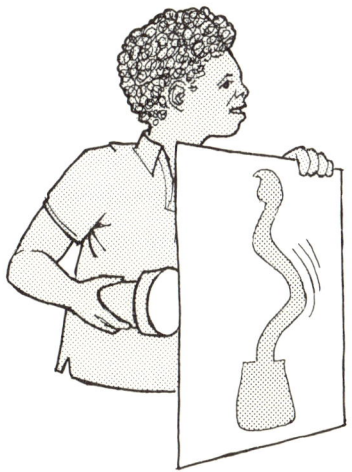

4. And now that your kids have the idea, invite them to use their black paper to make some kind of a long-necked, long-legged animal.

5. Staple the *body* of the cut-out animal to the white paper and raise the extremities so that the head, legs and tail will be able to "move."

Then, when the lights are off and the audience is ready—turn on your portable light, hold up your rear projection screens, and bring these creatures to life!

AND FINALLY:

If you *really* want to have some fun, see if you can dig up a copy of my third book, *Gene Baer's Wild and Wonderful Art Lessons* (Parker Publishing Co.: 1983), and take a good look at a lesson entitled *Hula Holiday!*

Lesson 9
Nose Art

You have just distributed the paste on squares of paper, and the art lesson is all set to go, when suddenly, a minor emergency arises making it necessary for you to attend to other matters "for a moment or two." So, what can you use in the meantime to keep your kids in their seats? Rope? A restraining order? Threats of capital punishment?

Here is one child-size diversion that succeeds every time. I call it *Nose Art!*

TO PRESENT:

"I'm going to be busy for a few minutes," you say to your class. "We'll get back to the art project in just a few minutes, but, in the meantime, here is your assignment:

"Draw a circle around your dab of paste, add ears, eyes, mouth, hair, but—best of all—shape the paste into a big honker. You know: a big fat nose, a long skinny carrot-like nose, a twisted nose, a beefy nose. *You* decide! And be sure to take your time to make it a good one, because I'm coming around in a few minutes to *inspect* your noses!*"

Now—do what you have to do, for by this time, your kids will already be gleefully at work!

---

* And if you want to raise the motivational level another notch, you can always put a twinkle in your eye and add the mock warning: "And be sure that *none* of these nose pictures ends up looking like *me!*"

Magical Improvizations

Lesson 10
The Magic Hexagon

If your kids find geometric figures b-o-r-i-n-g, perhaps they have never been properly introduced to the magic of mathematics.

Take, for example, the hexagon...

Basic Introduction to the Hexagon:

1. The easiest way to make a hexagon is to begin by drawing a circle with a pencil compass.*

2. Then, since each side of a hexagon is equal to the radius of the containing circle, simply use the same radius adjustment on your compass to divide the circumference into six equal parts.

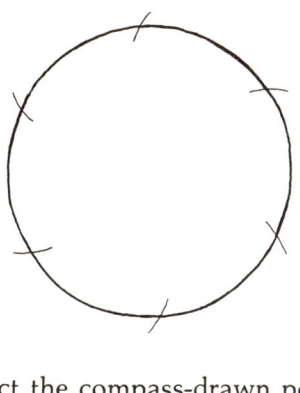

3. Connect the compass-drawn points, and that's that!

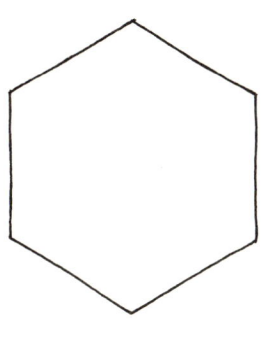

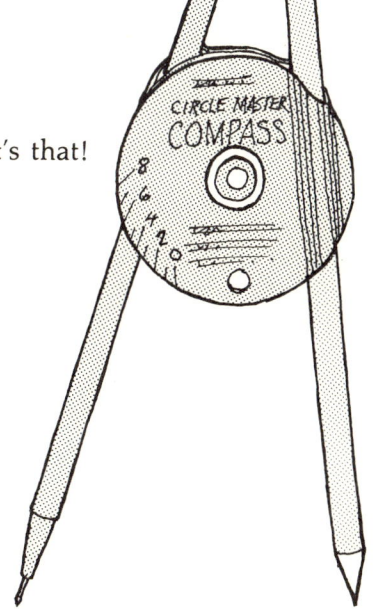

---

* In my opinion, the best all-around classroom compass is the Circle Master. It is easy to use, it is nearly indestructible, and it is manufactured by Educational Tools, Inc., 901 West Douglas, Wichita, Kansas 67213.

Activity 1: Putting the Hexagon Through Its Paces

EACH CHILD WILL NEED:

- pencil and paper
- a shared pattern (see *Preparations* below)
- a ruler or straightedge

PREPARATIONS:

Using tagboard (or other pattern-weight paperboard), prepare a number of hexagonal patterns for classroom use. Then, with the point of a pencil compass (or something similar), poke a hole into the exact center of each pattern, as shown here.

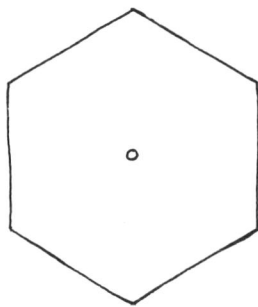

TO PRESENT:

Triangles and Hexagrams:

1. Place the pattern onto the paper in the "starting position" and trace only the points of the hexagon.

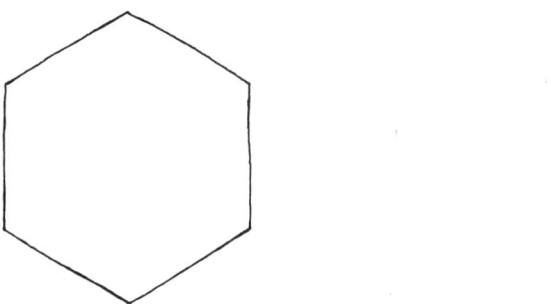 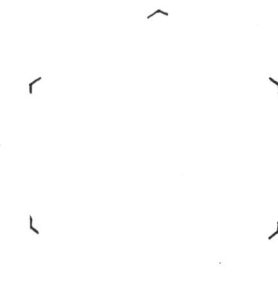

2. Invite your kids to "find out what would happen if you connected only every *other* point of a would-be hexagram."

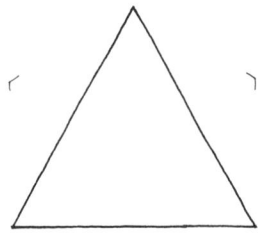

Magical Improvizations

3. Then, once everyone has drawn a triangle, invite your kids to connect the remaining three points to make a second triangle. The sum result: a hexagram!

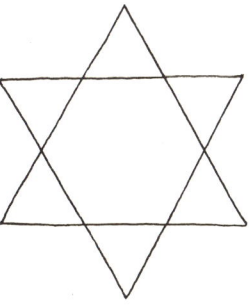

Boxed In!

Beginning again with the hexagonal pattern placed in the "starter position," have your kids trace four (or more!) complete hexagons with center holes. Then—when everybody is ready—use the chalkboard to lead your kids through the following exercises:

- Connect the points and a box appears!
- Add another line and the box is now open at one end!
- Or, open the box from one of its other visible sides.

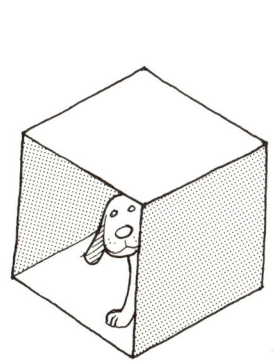
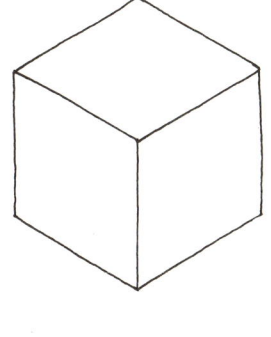

- *And finally*—draw the lines shown here and you have the beginnings of a house with a pointed roof!

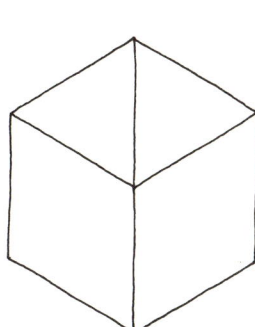

Activity 2: Hexaflowers

Here's one way to allow the hexagon to grow into a full-length lesson that your kids will love!

EACH CHILD WILL NEED:
- drawing paper
- shared patterns (see *Preparations*, page 141)
- pencils and crayons

TO PRESENT:

1. Invite your kids to trace their hexagonal patterns and to connect outside line segments to the center of the hexagon and complete with decorations.

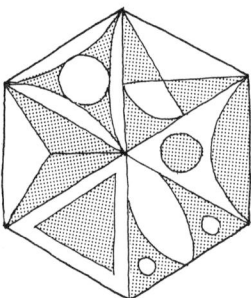
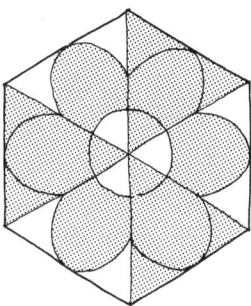

2. Add stems and leaves—and your classroom will bloom with the magic of geometry!

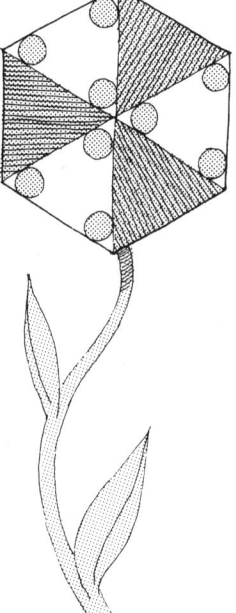

Magical Improvizations 145

Activity 3: Hexapatterns

One of the wonderful qualities of the hexagon is the way it interfaces with other hexagons.

EACH CHILD WILL NEED:

- drawing paper
- shared patterns (see *Preparations*, page 141)
- pencil and crayons

TO PRESENT:

Simply trace the patterns one against the other and begin!

Activity 4: A Gift for a Friend

Proof again of the versatility of the hexagon is this full-length lesson that begins as a hexagon and ends as a gift!

EACH CHILD WILL NEED:

- a shared hexagonal pattern (with center hole)
- drawing paper twice the length of the hexagonal pattern
- colored construction paper
- paste, pencils, scissors and crayons

TO PRESENT:

To Make the Gift:

1. Have your kids fold their drawing paper in half widthwise, place the edge of the hexagonal pattern against the fold of the paper and trace as shown here.

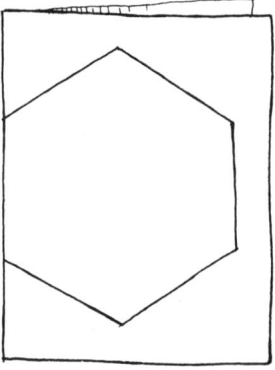

2. Cut out the hexagon through both thicknesses of the paper—*but do not cut on the fold.* The result will be as shown on the top of page 147.

Magical Improvizations

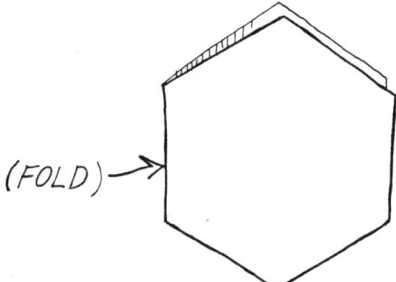

3. Add the three interior "box" lines and set this "gift box" aside for later.

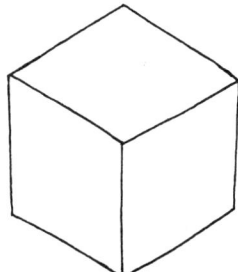

To Make the Ribbons: Now—using their hexagonal patterns as their guide—have your kids perform the following operations on their ribbon-colored construction paper:
 1. Trace the pattern, cut out the traced hexagon, and add the interior lines.

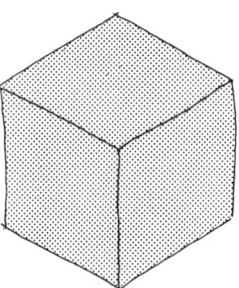

2. To make three V-shaped ribbon parts, remove the heavily shaded area and cut on the *newly* added lines shown here.

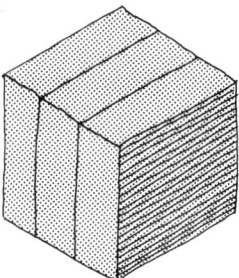

Then paste these three ribbon parts onto the card.

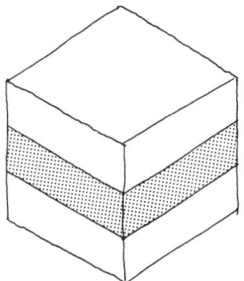 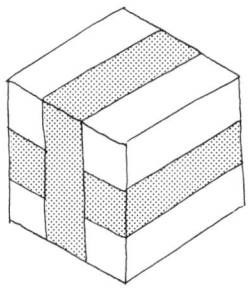 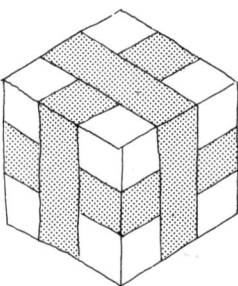

To Make the Bow: Cut two straight ribbon-width strips. Fold the first, and paste the second into a loop and from there into a bow as shown.

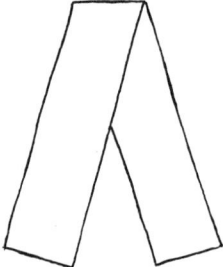 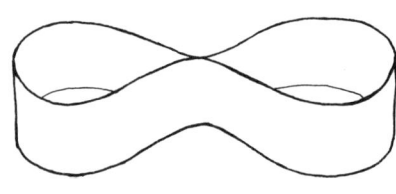

AND FINALLY:

Once the ribbons and bows have been assembled and pasted, invite your kids to use the inside of their cards to add whatever message—pictorial or otherwise—that would be appropriate to the occasion!

Lesson 11
Drawing by Magic

Here is a sampling of art tricks that are *proven* classroom entertainers!

Activity 1: Black and White Magic

Give a little kid a piece of carbon paper, and show this child what to do with it—and you have instantly made a friend!

Activity 2: Color Magic

Invite your kids to use a waxy crayon to make their own "carbon paper," or—better still—invite them to use *all* of their crayons to make a multi-colored transfer sheet.

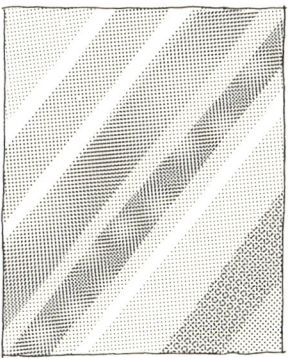

Activity 3: Transparent Magic

Many children have never seen tracing paper. Show them how to use it and you have opened their eyes a little wider!

Activity 4: Magic by Transference

Kids who are old enough to think that they know all that there is to know about tracing paper will be astounded to learn that a traced drawing can be transferred to another sheet of paper simply by turning a tracing face down and rubbing the back with a blunt instrument!

Activity 5: Heavy Metal

Here's a proven moneymaker. Try it and your kids will be enriched by the experience!

EACH CHILD WILL NEED:
- shared coins
- small squares of heavy foil
- a pencil with a rounded point
- scissors

TO PRESENT:

1. Invite your kids to press a square of foil around the top and sides of their coins. Then have them rub the foil gently with their pencil points to bring out the transferred detail.

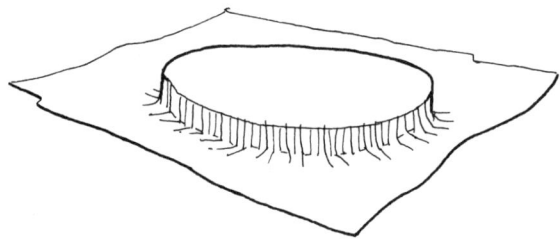

2. Cut away the excess foil and—faster than you can say "prison"—you are going to find yourself in the counterfeiting business!

Activity 6: White and Yellow Magic

EACH CHILD WILL NEED:
- white drawing paper
- pencil and crayons
- shared newspapers or comic books

Magical Improvizations

TO PRESENT:

1. Have your kids fold their drawing papers in half widthwise and use the top of this folded sheet to draw any kind of a picture in which T-shirts are featured. The only rule is this: the shirts should not be too small, and they should be colored in with a waxy layer of white or yellow crayon.

2. The completed picture is then turned over and held up to the light, or pressed against a classroom window, so that the main body of the T-shirt can be traced on the *back* of the paper.

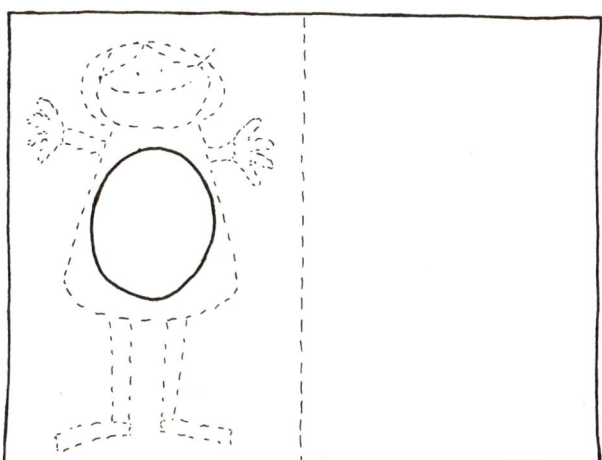

3. The folded paper is then reversed so that the drawing is on the inside and the penciled circle is on the outside.

Cartoons, roughly the size of the penciled circles, are then removed from newspapers or comic books—the brightly-colored Sunday comics are perfect for this activity!—and carefully positioned face up directly under the penciled circles. When this is done, simply invite your kids to use their pencils to color in the circled areas. (See illustration at the top of page 152.)

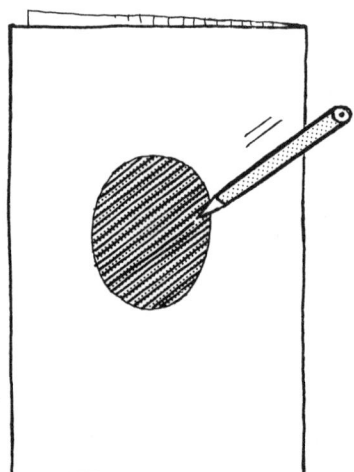

4. And that's it! When the penciling is done and the "books" are opened, your kids will be absolutely delighted to discover that their T-shirts have been "magically" decorated with a chosen cartoon!*

Activity 7: Newspaper Magic

EACH CHILD WILL NEED:

- a line drawing culled from the pages of your daily newspaper
- drawing paper
- a black fineline pen and assorted markers

TO PRESENT:

1. After your kids have placed their newspaper line drawing between the pages of a folded sheet of drawing paper, have them use their pencils to blacken the area directly above the picture to be transferred.

---

* Any lettering transferred in this process will (of course) appear in reverse; but since any unwanted parts of the transferred pictures can be scraped off, nothing has really been lost!

2. Open—and presto! A reverse image of the newspaper drawing will have appeared as if by magic. Sharpen up this image with markers and—"Wait 'till mother sees this!"

Lesson 12
Giving the Teacher a Hand!

In one of my earlier books,* I introduced a series of creative spurs under the title *Hand Starters*. Here are a few more of these wonderful hand creatures to add to your growing repertoire!

EACH CHILD WILL NEED:
- practice paper
- drawing paper
- pencil and crayons

---

* *Imaginative Art Lessons for Kids and Their Teachers*: Parker Publishing Company, Inc., West Nyack, New York.

GENERAL INSTRUCTIONS: (Borrowed from *Imaginative Art Lessons for Kids and Their Teachers, page 28 & 29*)

"Like a lot of other instructions for children, hand tracing directions are easy to give but sometimes difficult to follow. The best hand tracings are made when the pencil is held in a vertical position. With this simple observation in mind, the teacher can easily see—even at a distance—those children who have followed instructions and those who need additional reminders.

"The easiest way to present *hand starters* is simply to trace your own hand on the chalkboard and work along with kids. For more elaborate drawings, use a soft lead pencil and a sheet of white paper taped to the chalkboard or wall.

"Keep in mind that there is nothing sacrosanct about a *hand starter* (or, for that matter, any *starter!*), and that copybook perfection does not win the prize. Use these *hand starters* alone or in multiples as needed. Your job is simply to use whatever measure of guile necessary to ignite a child's imagination. Once your classroom's collective adrenalin is cooking on high heat, my best advice is to get out of the way and let their imaginations soar free . . ."

Activity 1: Hand Fish

1. Have your kids trace one of their hands,* but have them delete the tips of the three middle fingers.

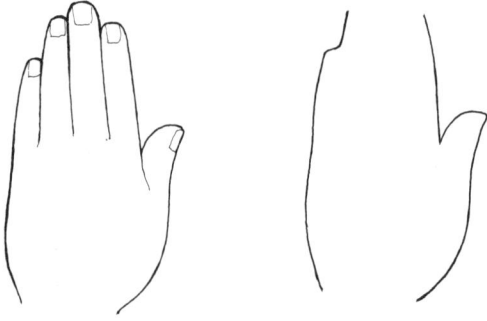

---

* These and the following hand-tracing instructions are for right-handed people. Lefties may find it more convenient to trace their other hand!

Magical Improvizations

2. Turn the paper and the rest is easy!

Activity 2: Hand Dog

1. Have your kids trace their hand as shown here.

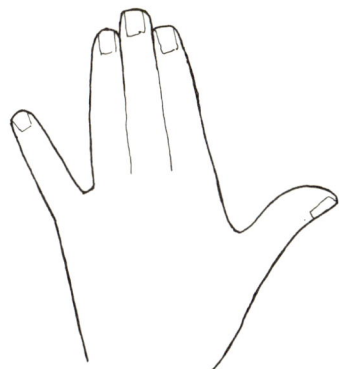

2. Turn the drawing upside down. The little finger and the thumb become the ears and the rest is self-explanatory!

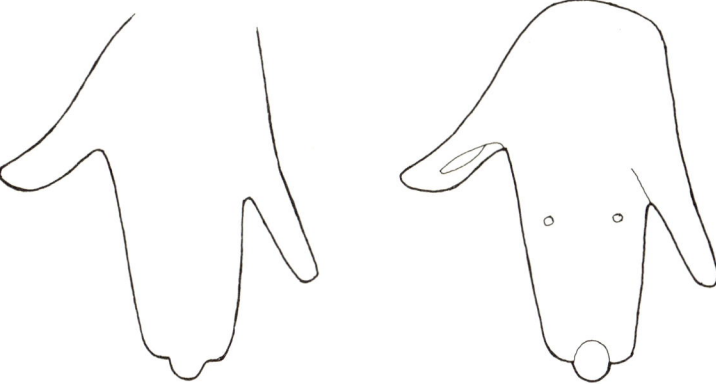

Activity 3: Uncle Harry

1. Have your kids trace their hand; but have them delete their fingertips.

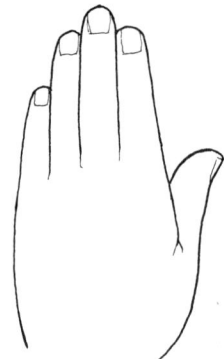

2. The tracing with the deleted fingertips is then turned upside down. The moment your kids understand that the thumb is the nose and the fingertips are the extremities of the beard, the instructions are over!

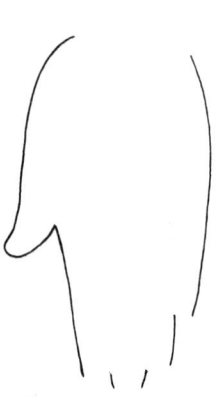 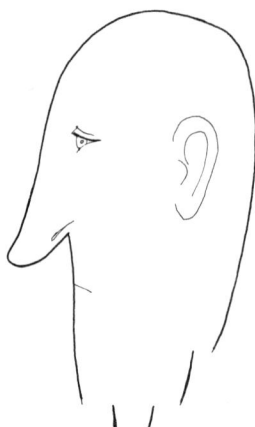 

Magical Improvizations

3. Bodies, of course, are optional.

Activity 4: A Pair of Nosy Characters

Here are a couple of brothers who live down our way. They call one "Beak" and the other "Pinocchio"—but you can call them anything you want!

To Make Brother "Beak":

1. Have your kids trace their hands in the position shown, with the index and forefinger tucked *halfway* under and the little finger tucked *all* the way under.

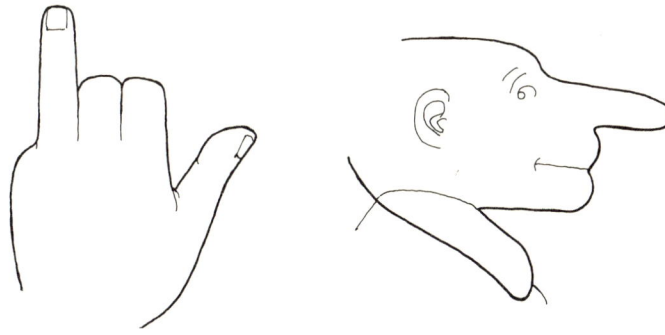

2. The tracing is then turned on its side—and the rest is easy!

To Make Brother "Pinocchio":

1. Have your kids trace their hands in the position shown; then invite them to turn their drawings thumb-side down.

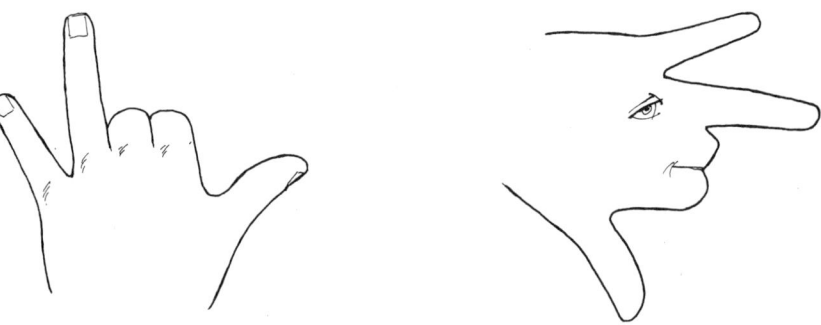

2. The primary difference between Pinocchio and his brother is that the little finger is used to make Pinocchio's hat brim, and the tucked-in fingers shorten the mouth area. Otherwise the family resemblance remains!

Activity 5: Mr. Big

1. Have your kids trace their hands in the position shown.

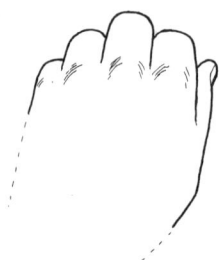

2. Then turn the paper so the traced hand is viewed, as shown at the top of the following page. The index finger becomes the nose, the tip of the thumb the forehead, and the rest is self-explanatory!

Magical Improvizations 159

Activity 6: Mrs. Handbag

1. Have your kids trace their hands as shown.

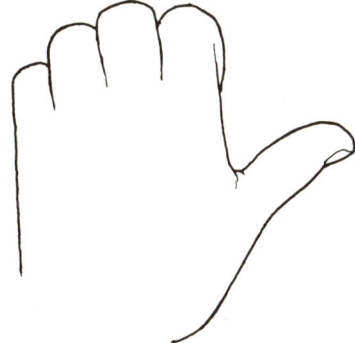

2. The little finger is to become the front of the hair; the ring finger, the forehead and the rest is easy!

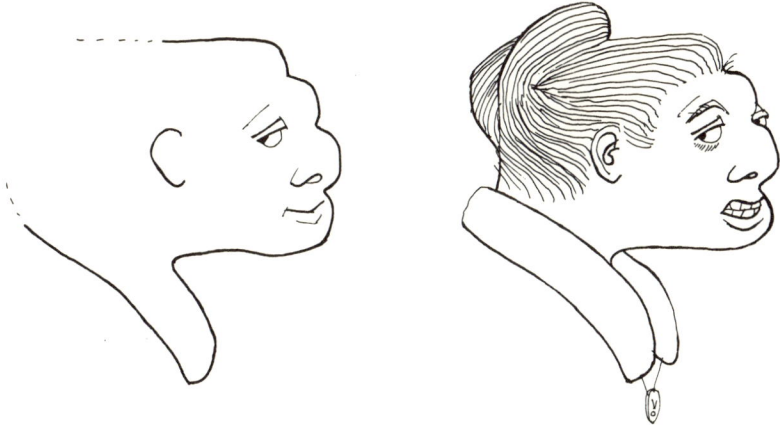

Activity 7: A Frantic Bird

1. Have your kids trace their hands, as shown, but trace only half the thumb.

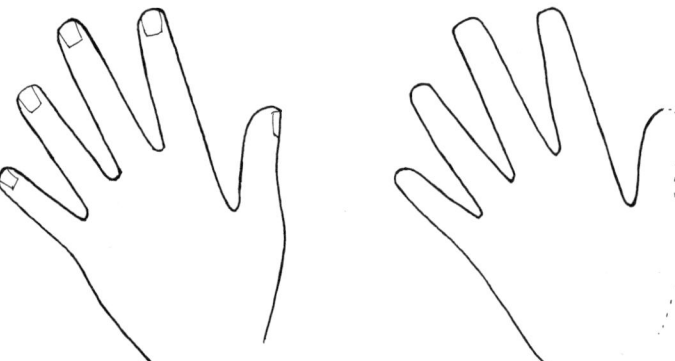

2. Then trace the other hand in the same way, in the overlapping position. Add a few more lines, make a few simple changes—and that's that!

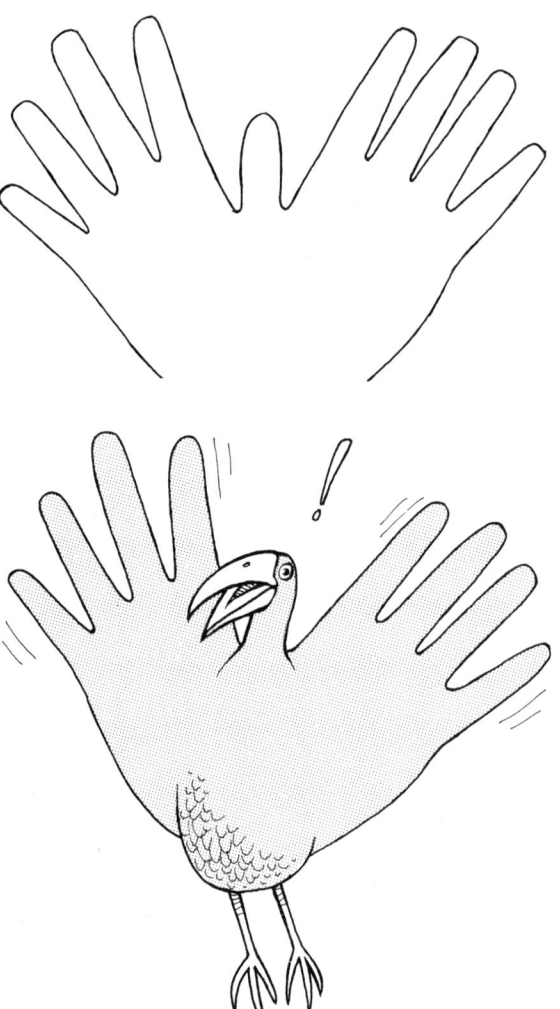

Magical Improvizations

Activity 8: Street Person

1. Have your kids trace their hands in the position shown.

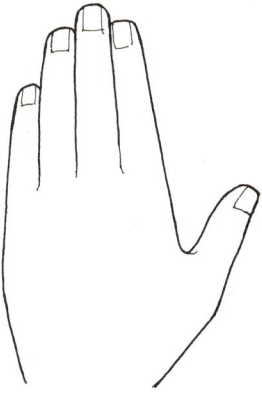

2. Turn the finished tracing upside down. And once your kids understand that the thumb is to become the arm, your job is over!

Activity 9: Some Handy People to Have Around

Here is a proportion system that is *always* on hand when you need it!

EACH CHILD WILL NEED:
- practice paper
- 12″ × 18″ drawing paper
- pencil and crayons

Magical Improvizations

TO PRESENT:

"This . . . " you explain to your class as you draw an ungainly-looking creature on your chalkboard, "is a weird-looking person! And yet—how would you explain to me what it is that's wrong with it?"

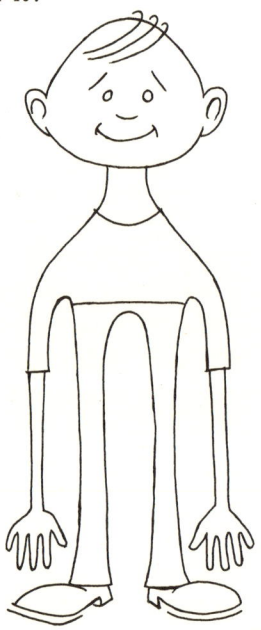

"The arms are too long!" After thanking your critics you shorten the arms. You appear puzzled. "But it *still* doesn't look right," you say as you turn back to your kids. "Anybody else have a suggestion?"

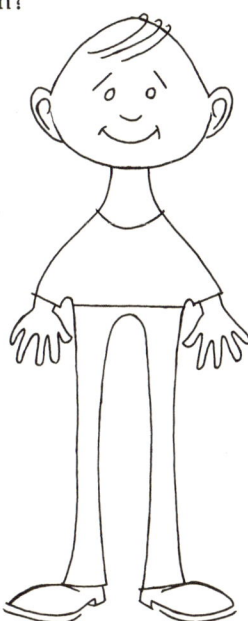

"The legs are too long!" So you shorten the legs and once again you shake your head. "But it *still* looks wrong!"

After additional suggestions are made and acted upon, you finally erase the drawing in mock despair. Turning to your class you say, "What was wrong with that drawing, at least from a realistic point of view, was that it was *out of proportion*—which is nothing more than a fancy way of saying that *everything* was the wrong size!

"So today," you explain, "I am going to show you one way of drawing people that works every time!"

Here's how:

1. With one hand placed on the practice paper in the position indicated, have your

kids trace the abbreviated outline. Only one additional suggestion is needed at this point: when tracing the fleshy area between the thumb and the first finger (see arrow), push in with the pencil so as to trim "a pound or two" of unwanted fat from this part of the outline.

2. Then turn the tracing upside down, add the other side of the body, and complete as suggested.*

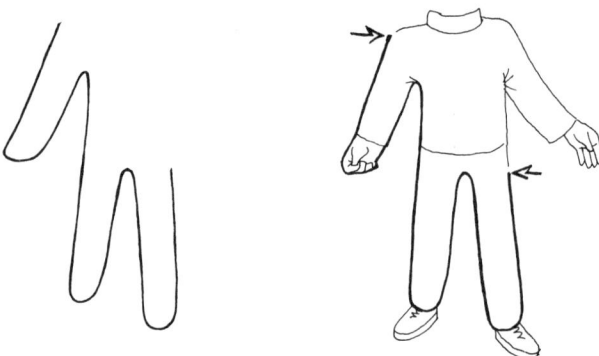

3. And the head? How big should the head be? Why, a head drawn the size of a thumb tip will supply the perfect answer!

AND FINALLY:

Just before you pass out the 12" × 18" drawing paper so that your kids can begin to explore the creative possibilities of these hand-made figures, climax your demonstration by showing your class some of the many ways in which these basic hand tracings can suggest a variety of useful occupations!

---

* No drawing system is perfect, and while these *Handy People* offer a quick and easy solution to the problems of approximating the proportions of the human body, they do tend to favor broad shouldered people! For this reason, it is best to advise your kids accordingly, so that they can reduce the width of the traced thumb as suggested in many of the figures that accompany this lesson.

Magical Improvizations 165

Lesson 13
Escape Artists

While this activity takes but a few minutes to perform, the results are often quite spectacular. Try it and you'll see what I mean!

EACH CHILD WILL NEED:
- 9" × 12" drawing paper
- tempera paint and a stiff brush
- two or three feet of string

Magical Improvizations   167

TO PRESENT:

1. Have your kids fold their papers in half, widthwise, and set these folded papers to one side.

2. Using the tempera paint and a stiff brush, have your kids paint their strings. Explain that the paint shouldn't be applied too heavily, and advise your kids to leave a "holding end" unpainted.

3. The painted part of the string is then dangled and the top half of the paper is lowered to make a "string sandwich". Now, while the "sandwich" is held loosely captive under the gentle pressure of one hand, the other hand pulls on the exposed string.

4. And that's it! Unfold the paper and see for yourself the tasteful art work which has been left behind by the escaping string!

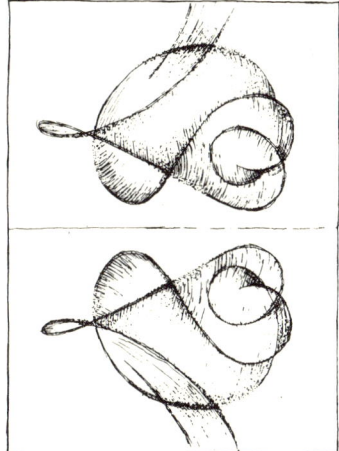

Separate the two halves, choose the better of the two, and mount with taste and dignity.

5. And if you agree with me that this is an activity worthy of further explorations, be sure to experiment with two or more strings in different colors!

Lesson 14
Origami Box and Water Bomb

The *Origami Box* has a long life and can be used repeatedly; the *Water Bomb* is a one-time celebration. The *Origami Box* can be handled with impunity; the *Water Bomb*, only with careful supervision.

Or—on second thought—you may *never* want to use the *Water Bomb* at all! *You* decide!

Activity 1: Origami Box

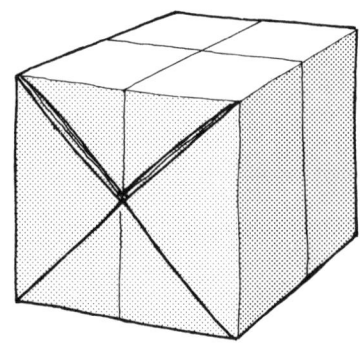

EACH CHILD WILL NEED:

- 8-1/2" × 11" lightweight paper (typing, mimeo, copier, etc.)
- scissors

TO PRESENT:

1. Have your kids prepare a 8-1/2" square from their 8-1/2" × 11" paper.*
2. The first four folds are identical to those used to begin the *Primary Banger* (page 122).
3. The folded packet should now look like the one shown here.

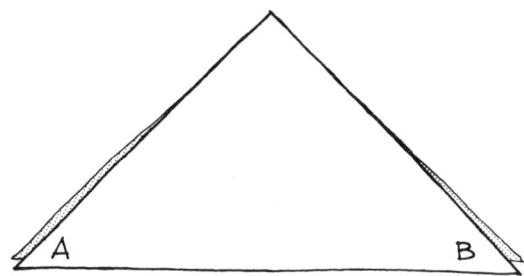

---

* See "Tricks, Shortcuts, Etcetera. . ." under *Sailboating* (page 198) for instructions on making a *Sailboat Square*.

Magical Improvizations

4. Follow the instructions given here:

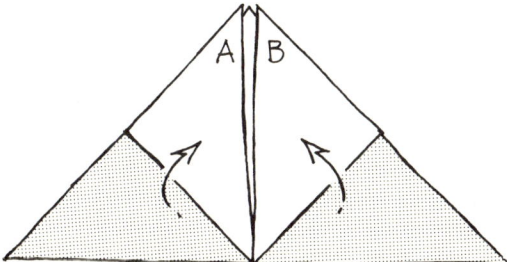
Fold corners A and B to apex.

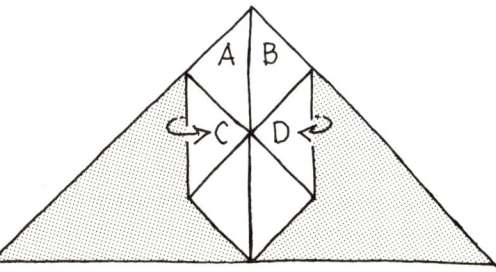
Fold new corners C and D to center.

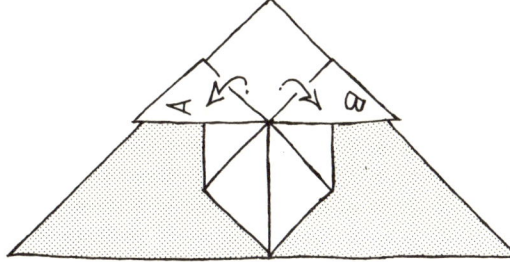
Fold A and B down and out.

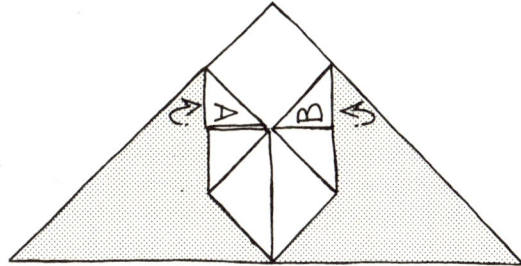
Fold A and B to center.

5. At this point, invite your kids to lift the flap formed to find the hidden lock pocket. Refold Flap A and insert same into the "hidden" pocket. Do the same with Flap B.

6. Turn this half-finished project face down and repeat this same series of folds on the reverse side. The folded packet will now look like the one shown at the top of the following page.

7. Fold on the dotted lines, and exercise these folds until they begin to lose their memory.

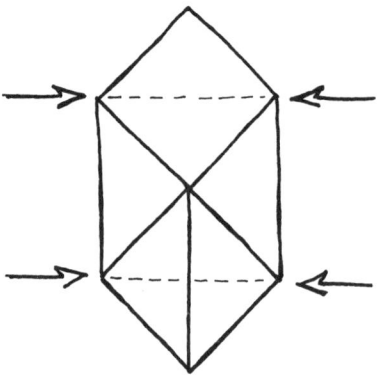

To Inflate: Only one end of this packet has an opening: find it. Blow into this open end and—presto!—a fullblown box will appear!

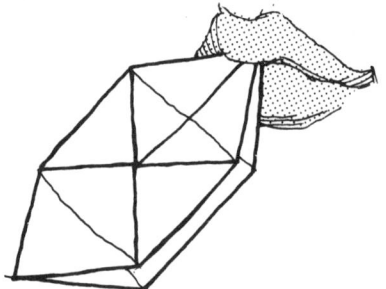

Activity 2: Water Bomb

After three days of showers the kids were desperately in need of something special to lift their rainsoaked spirits. Not knowing where else to turn, I reached for the Water Bomb . . .

Magical Improvizations

EACH CHILD WILL NEED:

- 8-1/2" × 11" lightweight paper (typing paper, duplicating, mimeo, copier, etc.)
- scissors
- a large washtub-size container and a smaller pot or pan

TO PRESENT:

1. Have your kids make an *Origami Box*. (See previous activity.)

2. Have a couple of your kids haul the washtub-size container outside and place it directly below one of your classroom windows. (Second-floor windows are ideal!)

3. The *Origami Boxes* are then filled with water, carried to the window (this is where the small pot or pan comes in), and each water-filled box is then gleefully hurled into the gaping mouth of the awaiting washtub . . .

4
Full-Scale Production Numbers

In this chapter, I am going to share with you some of my most cherished classroom "secrets." While none are short and all require *at least* two classroom sessions, they are easy to present, easy to do, and *all* lead to stunning conclusions.

Lesson 1
Black Magic

Like all teachers, I have my favorite art projects—and this *Black Magic* lesson is one of them. It's big, it's showy, and the results are always exquisite!

FOR EACH CHILD YOU WILL NEED:
- a pencil
- a sheet of heavy drawing paper or Bristol board
- crayons (*in*cluding white but *ex*cluding black)

YOU WILL ALSO NEED:
- a few bottles of India ink
- a few stiff brushes
- a Crayon Scraper*
- either lots of newspaper—or a stapler and a few sheets of large drawing paper

TO PRESENT:

Step One:

First of all, your kids will need a picture idea. Although the choice of subject matter is incidental to the success of this project (and should prove to be no obstacle to younger children), older children will always respond to a non-threatening "starter" idea such as the one that I am about to describe. I call it "The Creature That Never Was":

---
* See "Tricks, Shortcuts, Etcetera . . ." for paragraph on Crayon Scrapers (page 193).

"To begin with," you say to your class, "you need a picture idea: something big and something without a lot of fussy detail. My suggestion is this: use your paper and pencil to create some kind of a fantastic creature, one that no one, including yourself, has ever seen—ever!"

The advantage of using this kind of an approach as a starter is that by emphasizing the "fantastic" and de-emphasizing the "creature," you will free the "lousy dragon drawers" from the standards by which the "good dragon drawers" would like all others to be judged!

And with that—your lesson will be off to a good start.

Step Two:

Once the picture idea has been penciled in, instruct your kids to "color everything—*except the lines*—with a *heavy* coating of crayon." (The dotted lines shown here represent the pencil lines; the tone, the heavy layer of crayon that does not touch the lines.)

"Except the *lines*?"

And if your kids are like my kids, at this point they will probably look at you as if you're speaking Mandarin. For this reason, I suggest that you back up your verbal instructions with some sort of a visual explanation, either one manufactured on the spot, or one prepared beforehand.

Question: "But what's this about pressing down hard with our crayons? What if I want a *light* green sky? How can I have a light green sky if I have to press down hard with my regular old grass-green crayon?"

Answer: "Your sky can be as light as green meringue, but since it must also be covered with a heavy coating of wax—this is where the white crayon comes into play. Simply cover your light green sky with a topping of white, and the problem is solved!"

Question: "And another thing. Since I want this creature's eyeballs to be white, what do I do—just leave them white?"

Answer: "Since everything except the lines have to be covered with a heavy layer of crayon, it follows that if you want white eyeballs—then you are going to have to color them white!"

Question: "And why can't I use my black crayon?"

Answer: "For reasons too complicated to explain at this moment, black crayons are out. But there *is* a good reason. Trust me! You'll see!"

Question: "Whoops! I made a mistake. I colored a line. Now what do I do?"

Answer: "That's what the Crayon Scrapers* are for."

Question: "That's what I'm using, but the crayon still doesn't come all the way off. What do I have to do now? Start all over again?"

Answer: "If you have removed the crayon *wax* and there is still a crayon *stain* left behind, then don't worry about it. The crayon stain will disappear in Step Three!"

Step Three:

Once the coloring is complete, have your kids paint their pictures with a wash of India ink but, before you do so, be sure to read the information contained in the following paragraphs:

- One of the ironies of this project is that the more conscientious the artist, the more scrubbing it will take to get the ink to cover the crayon. In any case, the layer of ink need not completely obliterate the buried image in order to "work." As long as the ink covers the entire picture—that's all that's expected here!
- Impatient inkers are often inclined to hurry the painting process by using too much ink. Since any puddles left to dry may prove troublesome later on, this part of the project may demand a little supervision.
- When the inking is done, stop, for it is important that the pictures be *thoroughly* dry before you proceed to Step Four.
- And now, for some bad news. It is impossible to paint over crayon without also peppering the India ink with crayon crumbs. For this reason I suggest that when the last child finishes with Step Three, you put an appropriate label on these bottles and store them separately from any uncontaminated inks that you might have on hand.

Step Four:

Once the ink is dry it is then scraped off with a Crayon Scraper. Here are a few helpful suggestions:

---

* See "Tricks, Shortcuts, Etcetera . . ." for paragraph on Crayon Scrapers (page 193).

- Since the black streaks left behind by the scraping process are also art elements that make a considerable contribution towards the success of this project, advise your kids *"not to scrap it all off"*!
- The scraping is best done in parallel strokes. The most comfortable stroke for "righties" is a right-to-left, downwardly slanting stroke; for "lefties," a downward stroke in the opposite direction.
- While the mess accompanying Step Four may not be immediately obvious, the unwanted by-product here is the tiny slivers of crayon scrapings that stick to nearly everything they touch. Here are a couple of suggestions to help you keep this mess to a minimum:
  - If you have a couple of extra classroom desks, cover them with newspapers and set them off to one side where the scrapings can be kept at arm's length from the rest of the room.
  - Or do as I do and make a few utility boxes* from large sheets of drawing paper. These paper boxes will not only effectively contain the pesty scrapings but they have the additional advantage of being cheap and disposable. (I like the "disposable" feature best of all!)

AND FINALLY:

Although I am a veteran teacher who has seen a lot of lesson plans come and go, I can think of no other art project that has consistently produced the uniformly high quality of finished art as this Black Magic production number.

After reading a recommendation as glowing as *that*—don't you think that this *Black Magic* lesson is worth at least a try?

Lesson 2
Pencil Pointillism

You've found enough tempera paint in your closet to have your kids enjoy some kind of a painting project, but unless you can remember where you stored the brushes, the whole idea will have to be shelved.

Or will it?

EACH CHILD WILL NEED:

- 9" × 12" drawing paper, heavy enough to take tempera
- tempera paint (red, yellow, blue, and white will do just fine!)
- a pencil for drawing
- an unsharpened classroom-style pencil with an attached eraser

TO PRESENT:

1. Invite your kids to use their "drawing" pencil and paper to sketch out some kind of a picture idea that will not require a great deal of detail.

---

* See "Tricks, Shortcuts, Etcetera . . ." for paragraph on Utility Boxes (page 192).

Full-Scale Production Numbers

2. Discuss the whole idea of pointillism with your kids and, if possible, show them a print or two of a painting by Seurat.

3. And that's it! The rest is simple. Just invite your kids to use the eraser end of their unsharpened pencil as a painting tool!

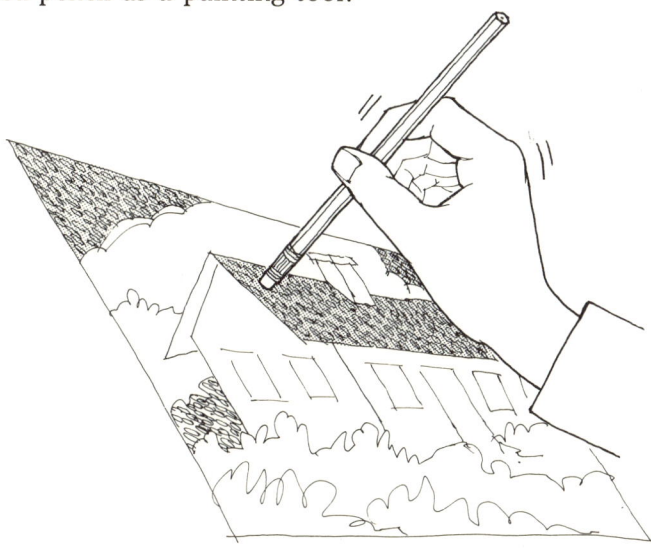

Further Comments and Suggestions:

1. If you limit the selection of paints to the primary colors plus white (and possibly black), you will have arranged the conditions for a lot of hands-on learning about the nature of color.

Yellow + red = orange
Red + blue = purple
Blue + yellow = green
Red + yellow + blue = brown

2. After your kids have completed their pictures, collect the pencils, wash off the paint, and return the pencils to your desk drawer. In this way, today's painting tools can become tomorrow's writing instruments!

Lesson 3
Full-Color Journalism

If you have been looking for a couple of lessons that will guarantee *spectacular* results—look no further!

Activity 1: Full-Color Transparencies

EACH CHILD WILL NEED:

- 8-1/2" × 11" drawing paper

- 8-1/2" × 11" acetate (such as that used for overhead projectors) and a black permanent marker or transparency marker with a reasonably sharp point.
- an illustrated magazine (the classroom *National Geographics* will do just fine!)
- construction paper in assorted colors and sizes
- paste and scissors

PREPARATIONS:

Staple each sheet of acetate to a sheet of drawing paper.

TO PRESENT:

1. Invite your kids to look over their magazines until they "find a picture worth tracing." Once a suitable picture has been found, have your kids sandwich the chosen picture between the pre-stapled acetate and drawing paper, and then make a detailed tracing using their black markers. The undamaged magazine can then be returned to the classroom library.

2. Now comes the fun part as this dull tracing begins to undergo a series of kaleidoscopic changes:

Begin by having your kids insert a sheet of colored construction paper between the drawing paper and the acetate tracing and watch their faces as the black line seems

to magically rise from the surface of the drawing paper to transfer itself to the corresponding surface of the colored construction paper!

3. Then, after your kids have had ample opportunity to experiment with a variety of colored backgrounds, invite them to choose the colored sheet that best captures the mood of their pictures and to use this color as the field upon which to experiment with added scraps of cut or torn paper.

4. And when everyone is happy with their color arrangements, invite your kids to paste the cut and torn paper scraps into place. Trim, mount, and—admire!

Activity 2: Coloring the News

Although this second lesson takes considerably longer to complete than the first, the results are well worth the effort!

EACH CHILD WILL NEED:

- a black and white newspaper photograph (see *Preparations* for this lesson)
- lightweight drawing paper (typing paper, duplicating, mimeo, copier, etc.)
- white drawing paper or (even better) Bristol board
- pencil
- fineline black marker
- watercolors

THE TEACHER WILL NEED:

- stapler
- paper cutter (or shears)

PREPARATIONS:

The hardest part of this lesson is finding a suitable selection of clearly printed newspaper photographs which are interesting enough to be attractive to children; but once you have clipped out a sufficient number of these black and white photographs to allow for a selection from which your kids can choose, the rest will all fall easily into place!

TO PRESENT:

1. It's *your* job to staple each photograph to a sheet of lightweight drawing paper and to trim it so the stapled unit looks something like the one shown here.

2. This stapled unit is then opened, and the back of the lightweight drawing paper is then blackened with a vigorous application of pencil lead.

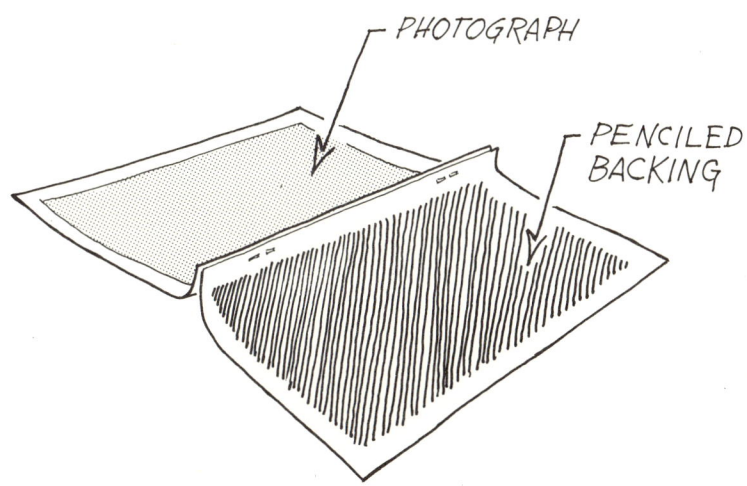

3. The stapled unit is stapled, in turn, to a sheet of white drawing paper (or Bristol board) and the kids are then invited to trace their photographs to the drawing paper via their homemade "carbons!"

4. Once the tracing is completed, the papers are separated, the "carbon" is thrown away, and the "good" paper is ready for painting!

Painting Instructions: Carefully explain to your kids that the watercolors are only for *painting*—that all *outlining* will be done at a later time with the help of a fineline marker.

AND FINALLY:

That's it! Paint, let dry, outline, mount and—display with pride!

Lesson 4
Washouts!

Despite its name, this lesson is very definitely one of the best; try it, and you'll see what I mean!

EACH CHILD WILL NEED:

- heavy drawing paper or, preferably, Bristol board
- pencil
- white tempera paint and a pointed brush
- India ink and a larger brush
- paper towel

THE TEACHER WILL NEED:

- a room with running water

TO PRESENT:

1. Invite your kids to sketch out some kind of a picture or design idea, such as the one suggested here, that does not involve a lot of detail.

2. When the sketches are complete, have your kids use their white tempera to paint everything *except* the lines.

Since these instructions require an enormous act of faith on the part of the student ("Paint a white picture *white*? Why? It's *already* white!"), this step of the lesson may initially require a lot of good-natured assurance that you *do* know what you're doing!

3. Once Step 2 has been completed and the paint has had a chance to dry, invite your kids to use the larger of their two brushes to paint the white picture with a wash of India ink. ("First we paint a *white* picture *white*," mutters one kid, "then we paint it black. I can't believe we're doin' this!")

4. But once the India ink is dry and your kids are gathered around the sink, the expectations will suddenly begin to rise.

You turn on the water and—one at a time—you invite your kids to place their blacked-out pictures directly under the open faucet where—like magic—a "miracle" will take place as the black pictures turn first gray and then white with emerging black lines!

Pat dry with paper towel and—congratulations, teacher—you've done it again!

Further Suggestions:

1. A light rubbing with the fingers over the washing *Washout* will hasten the transformation, but this rubbing should be done with great care since many washouts are improved by removing them from their bath and patting them dry before *all* of the black ink has been washed away!

2. And now that your kids have experienced the excitement of their first washout, why not try a colored one?

Do it; you'll love it!

Lesson 5
Sawing a Head in Half

Not that there is anything wrong with the traditional papier-mâché piggy banks and piñatas, but *Sawing a Head in Half* makes for twice the fun and half the mess!

YOUR CLASS WILL NEED:

- plenty of newspapers, paper towels, etc.
- one balloon for every two children
- paste (see *Preparations*)
- containers for paste and/or water
- masking tape
- paint and brushes
- paper cutter

PREPARATIONS:

1. *Choosing the Paste.* What kind of paste is best for papier-mâché? Read on and decide for yourself!

Kitchen Paste:

"Kitchen paste" is made from ordinary flour and water. Just mix the two together until the consistency is right for your needs—and that's that! Kitchen paste is perfect for classroom papier-mâché projects.

Wallpaper Paste:

The same paste that holds your wallpaper to the walls is also an excellent paste for papier-mâché. Wallpaper paste is considerably more expensive than kitchen paste, but for those of you who want to travel first class, this is the way to go! Just follow the directions on the side of the package.

Jar Paste:

While a *good* brand of jar paste *can* be used for papier-mâché, I would advise against it: on the other hand, a *cheap* brand can often be used to good advantage. Just use it straight from the jar!

Conclusion: Unless you have access to a windfall supply of wallpaper paste, you would be best advised to mix your own paste from flour and water—and save the jar paste for small projects or classroom emergencies.

2. *Preparing the Paper Strips.* Cut the strips on your paper cutter. As to size, the rule here is easy to remember: the smaller the strips, the smoother the surface. In any event, for most classroom work, I would advise against using strips much larger than 1″ × 6″.

3. *Applying Papier-Mâché to an Inflated Balloon.* To cover a balloon with strips of pasted paper is not one of the world's most difficult assignments. However, there are a few tricks worth knowing:

- Balloons being balloons, one should always begin with the knowledge that a certain amount of shrinkage will take place before the project reaches completion. To guard against the damage that a shrinking balloon could do to the surface of the papier-mâché, the best strategy is to apply the first layer of paper strips using *water* only. Then, once a few layers of paper *and* paste have been applied and the "egg" has been given a chance to dry, the internal support of the balloon is no longer crucial to the success of the project. So if the balloon wants to shrink—let it!

- When using wallpaper or kitchen paste, simply dip the paper strips into the bowl of paste, wipe off the excess and apply. When using jar paste, rub the paste on both sides of the strip and apply in the same manner.

- To guard against an uneven buildup of papier-mâché, the best rule is to apply alternate layers of different papers: a layer of black and white newsprint, a layer of full-color Sunday comics, a layer of paper towel, etc. This procedure will allow your kids to easily monitor their own progress.

- The paste and paper buildup of these masks is not something that can be accomplished in one period, so allow for a generous number of pasting sessions leisurely punctuated with plenty of drying time in between.

TO PRESENT:

1. Divide your class into pairs. If there should happen to be an odd number of children—guess who's elected to fill the missing position?

2. When the layers of papier-mâché have reached the point where it is determined that they are strong enough to withstand a little heavy handling, set the "eggs" aside to thoroughly dry for the last time.

3. The dried "eggs" are then sawed or cut in half lengthwise and each co-worker takes a half.*

4. From here on out, the lesson becomes a mask-making project. Crumpled balls of paper are taped on to make noses and then covered with papier-mâché; eyes are cut out, etc., and the finished mask is painted to taste!

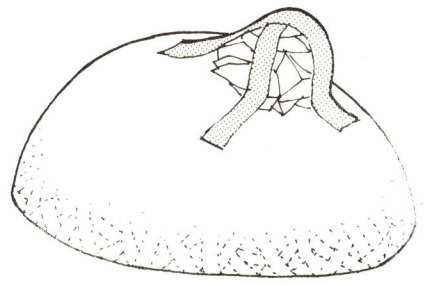

Lesson 6
Geodesic Creations

From garden sheds to stadiums, the structural strength of the triangle has proven itself to be second to none. While our *Creations* will be scaled to the classroom, the concept is large enough to encompass the horizon.

And what teacher could ask for a better beginning than that?

EACH CHILD WILL NEED:

- shared 3-1/2 (±) circle patterns (see *Preparations*)
- assorted colors of construction paper
- pencils and scissors
- shared staplers (Round up as many staplers as you can find—the more the better!)

PREPARATIONS:

Using tagboard (or other pattern-weight paperboard), prepare a number of circle patterns with paired cardboard triangles of corresponding size.

---

* Ragged edges can be corrected with tape or with additional papier-mâché.

If you need help in making these matching triangles, turn to page 194 to the section entitled *Equilateral Triangles* and follow Steps 1 and 2.

All points of the completed triangle, when centered on the circle pattern, should just touch the circumference of the paired circle as shown here.

TO PRESENT:

1. Once the circle patterns have been traced onto the construction paper and cut out with scissors, have your kids trace their triangles and fold.

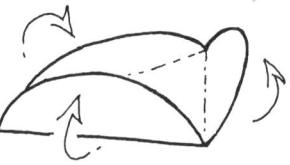

2. And from here on out, it is simply a matter of assembling and stapling!

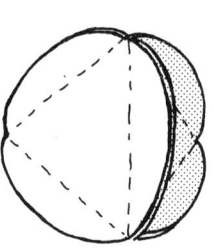
4 units (Three on top; one under)

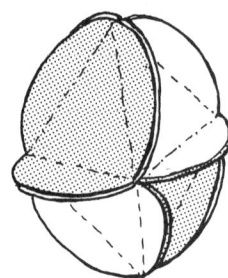
6 units (Two sets of three)

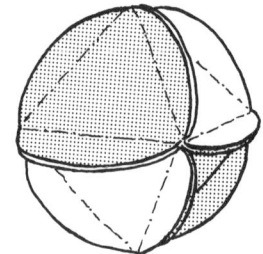
8 units (Two sets of four)

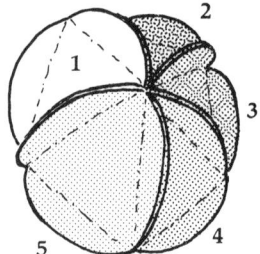
10 units (Two sets of five assembled clamshell-style)

Assembling Instructions for The Geodesic Stadium (15 Units)

1. Assemble five units as shown.

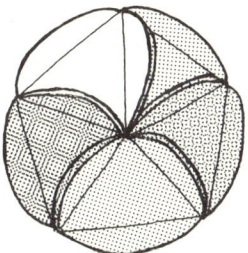

2. Staple another unit to each of the free flaps shown in the figure accompanying Step 1.

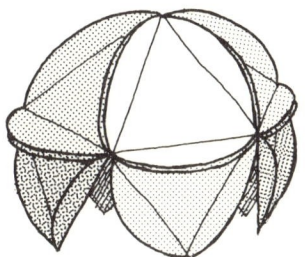

3. Staple another unit between each of the units added in Step 2. Turn it bowl-side down and comtemplate!

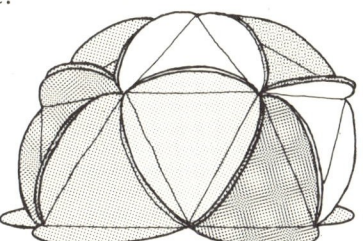

Assembling Instructions for The Geodesic Sphere (20 Units)

Following the instructions given in Steps 1 and 2 of the preceding activity (the Geodesic Stadium), have your kids assemble two of the saw-toothed hemispheres pictured in Step 2 of the Geodesic Stadium. These two halves are then fitted together and stapled to complete the finished assembly. Admire as is or hang from the ceiling for everyone to applaud!

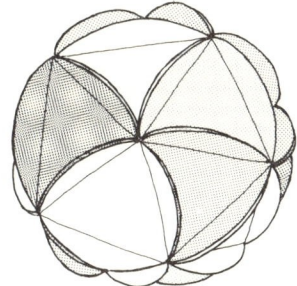

Lesson 7
The Greatest Showstopper of Them All!

And just about the time that your kids are beginning to think that they have seen *everything*—maybe it's time to "leave them laughing" with *The Greatest Show Stopper of Them All!*

YOUR CLASS WILL NEED:

- brushes
- tempera paint
- markers

THE TEACHER WILL NEED:

- a cardboard box
- a sharp knife (see *Preparations*)

PREPARATIONS:

Cut out one side of a cardboard box to make a puppet stage with a proscenium opening that is more or less equal to the distance of a child's arm from the tip of the extending fingers to a few inches above the child's wrist.

The cardboard theater can be as simple and unadorned as that shown in the left figure or as elaborate as the one shown at the right. (*Your* choice!)

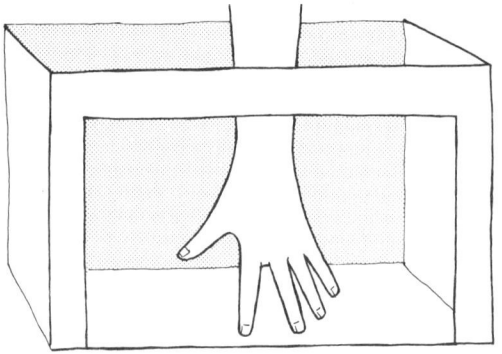

OPTIONAL PREPARATIONS:

Presentation styles differ, but the way I have always presented this lesson is a proven crowd pleaser. Here's what I do:

Just before class time, I closet myself away from prying eyes just long enough to transform my hand into a living puppet (see *Puppet-Making Instructions*). Then, when the paint is dry, I slip my puppet hand into a sweater, slacks, or jacket pocket where it can "sleep" until needed.

Then, once my class has been assembled long enough for me to remind them that today is National Puppet Day ("What? You didn't listen to the President's speech last night?"), I invite my absent puppet to introduce itself to the class. At that, the "missing" puppet jumps out of my pocket, performs a little dance on a neighboring desk, and then disappears into my pocket again!

The reception given this startling guest appearance is always one of spontaneous delight. To cries of "Let's see it again!" your puppet jumps onto another desk and then hurriedly leaps back again into your pocket. This is repeated until everyone is "psyched up" to a point where they would rather forfeit their own birthday parties than miss the chance of making their own flesh and blood puppets.

Then—you are ready to begin!

Puppet-Making Instructions

The Head. Invite your kids to use their markers and tempera paint to transform their wrist (or the wrist of another) into a head by *drawing* the face and *painting* the hair. (Note that one of the remarkable features of these puppets is each comes with its own distinctive skin color!)

The Body. The rest is more or less self-explanatory. The index and middle finger become the legs, the hand becomes the body, and the thumb becomes one arm. The little finger and the ring finger are tucked out of sight so that the "other arm" can be positioned as shown, with the "hand" drawn on the knuckle of the ring finger!

AND FINALLY:

Bring out your puppet stage and let your kids celebrate their own creativity! *Enjoy!*

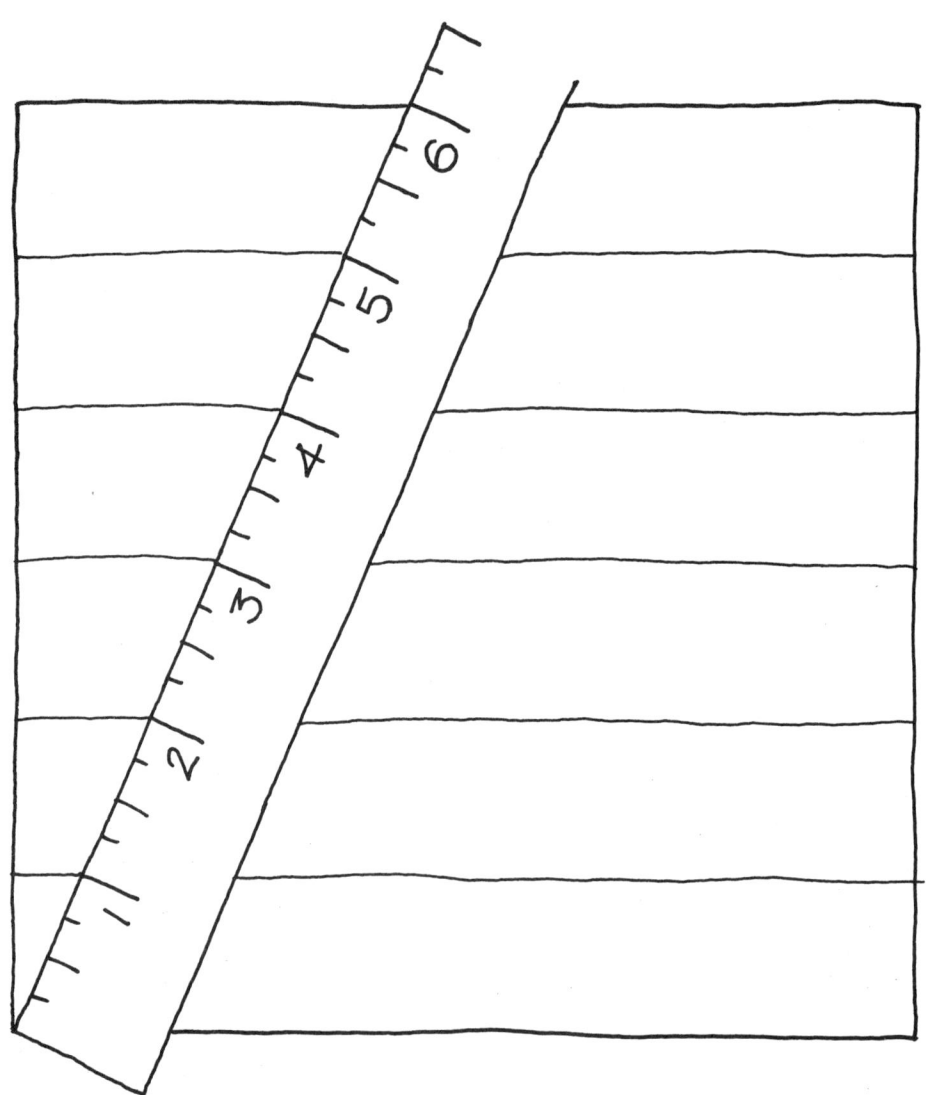

5
Tricks, Shortcuts, Etcetera...

BOX MAKING

While the paper box has its structural limitations, it is nevertheless capable of performing an endless variety of friendly chores. Here are two of my favorites:

The Sixteen-Part Box

1. Fold the paper in half widthwise, unfold, and then fold the short sides to the middle as shown.

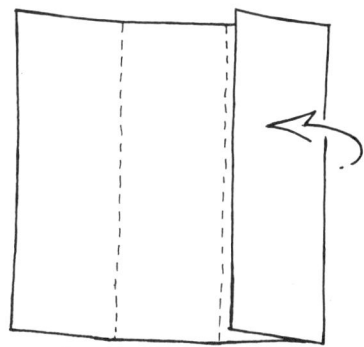

2. Repeat this same series of folds lengthwise and cut on the heavy lines.

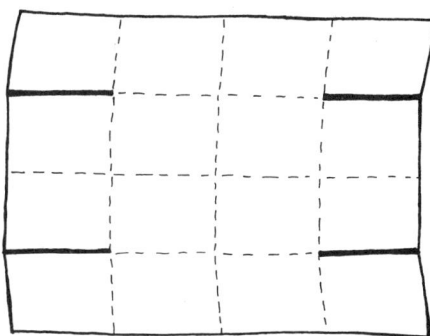

3. The large, center end flaps are turned up, the side flaps are turned in, and the extending flap is folded over and secured as shown in the illustration at the top of the next page.

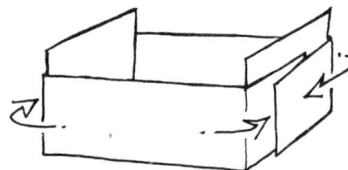 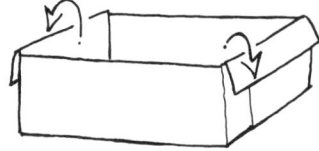

The Utility Box

Nothing could be easier: fold up all four sides of a sheet of paper, pinch the corners on the diagonal, and staple!

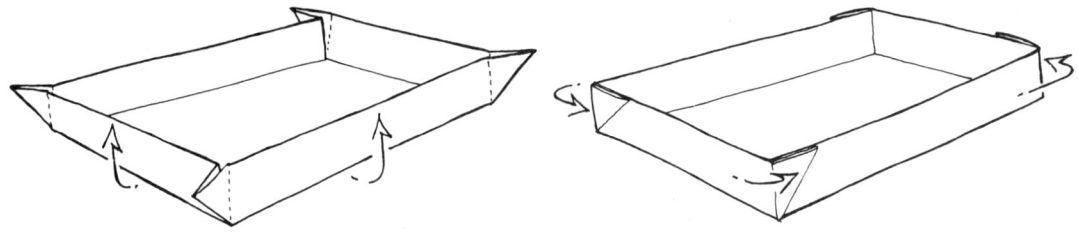

CIRCLECONES*

To Make a Circlecone from a Circle:

1. Draw a line from the center of the circle to the edge and cut on this line.

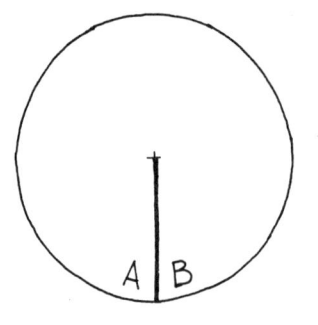 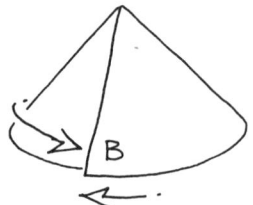

2. Overlap A with B and paste!

To Make a Circlecone from a Half Circle:

Simply paste A to B as shown.

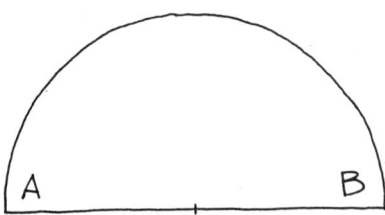 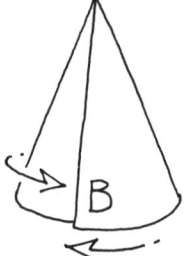

---

* Those who are familiar with my previous books will note that I have simplified the terminology here by broadening the definition of the term *Circlecone* to encompass similar operations performed without circles or circle segments.

Tricks, Shortcuts, Etcetera...

To Circlecone a Rectangular Sheet of Paper:
Overlap corners A and B. Paste!

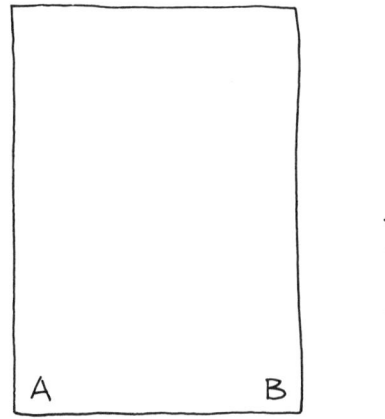 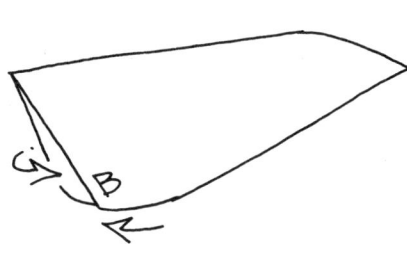

CRAYON SCRAPERS

For classroom purposes, a "good" **crayon scraper** is any tool (such as a dull knife) that "does the job." For a perfect crayon scraper, however, you need a *round-ended scraper*, a metal artists' tool such as the one shown here which fits into a standard penholder.

EGGS AND OVALS

This is as good a place as any to explain away some of the mysteries of egg and oval making.

Here's how:

The Egg

Fold a sheet of paper lengthwise and draw half an egg against the fold. Cut out this egg shape through the double thickness of the folded paper. Open and contemplate. Refold, make whatever corrections are necessary, and open again.

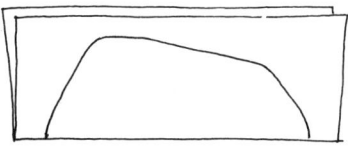 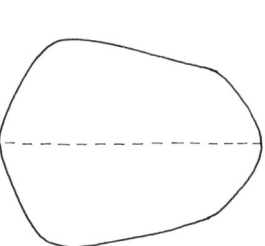 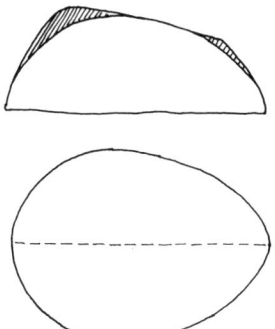

The Oval

1. Fold a sheet of paper in half lengthwise and then widthwise.

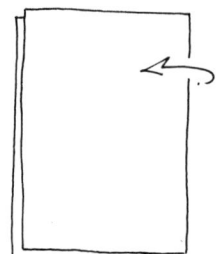 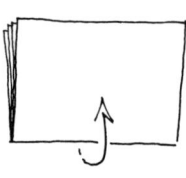

2. The rest is nothing more than a simple trial and error operation. Draw a curved line and cut on this line through all four thicknesses of the paper.

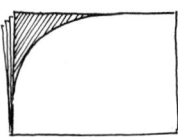

3. Open and contemplate. If it is not the oval of your dreams, refold and make corrections!

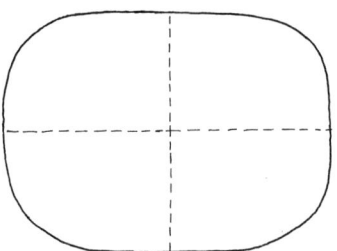 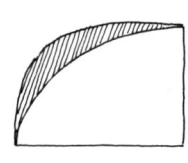 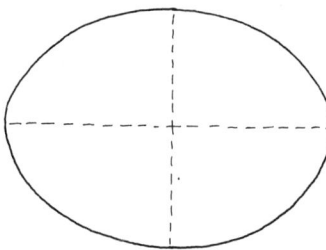

EQUILATERAL TRIANGLES

There are, of course, ways to make equilateral triangles other than that shown in the method described below; but this is the one that is best suited for our needs.

To Make an Equilateral Triangle that Will Fit Perfectly Inside Its Parenting Circle:

1. Take the radius of a circle for a walk around its circumference, and the result will be a circle divided into six equal parts.

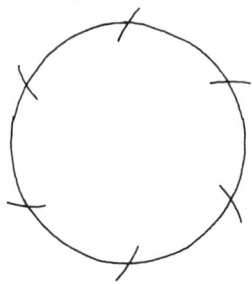

Tricks, Shortcuts, Etcetera... 195

2. Connect every other division mark with a straight line—and that's that!

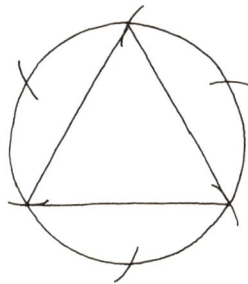

For a further study of equilateral triangles and their parenting hexagons, be sure to see the *Magic Hexagon* lesson that begins on page 141.

MEASURING STRIPS, STRAIGHTEDGES, AND RULERS

Measuring Strips

A measuring strip is nothing more than a piece of tagboard (or other pattern-weight paperboard) cut to a pre-measured width. If, for example, you would like to have your kids divide a 9" square into nine 3" squares, you can either dig out your battered rulers and hope for the best, or you can hand out freshly-cut 3" × 9" tagboard measuring strips and show your kids how to quickly and easily perform this same task in seconds!

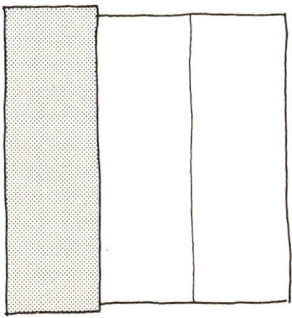

Straightedges

I could write a long comic essay on all of the reasons I prefer not to use rulers for art projects, but instead I will simply recommend strips of tagboard (or other pattern-weight paperboard) as an inexpensive and readily available instrument for drawing straight lines.

Rulers

Here are three ruler tricks that are well worth the knowing.

Ruler Trick 1: How to Divide Any Length into a Given Number of Equal Parts

Just for the sake of simplicity, let's assume that you would like to divide a 5-1/2" square into six equal parts. Now you can either turn to your math and begin to divide 5-1/2" into 6—or you can do as I do:

1. Place the end of the ruler on one side of the paper and a number easily divisible by 6 on the other.

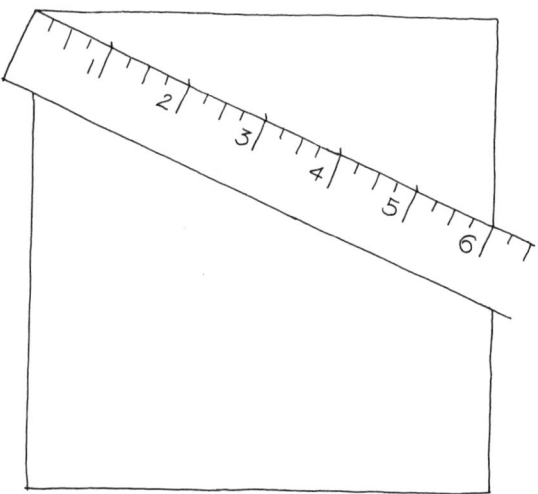

2. Draw vertical lines through these marked-off measurements and your job is done!

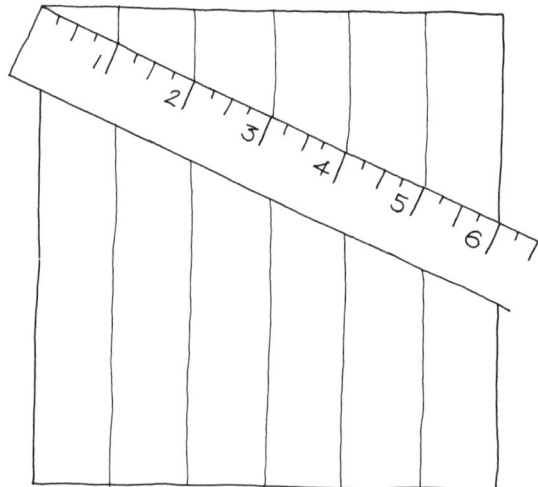

Ruler Tricks 2 and 3: How to Divide Any Length into Two Equal Parts

While Trick 1 is perfect for finding multiple divisions of equal length, there are easier ways to divide a given distance into *two* equal parts.

First Method The width of your posterboard is 23-13/16" and you need to find the center. Half of 23-13/16" is . . . ?

Cut a paper strip equal in length to the given width, fold the strip in half, open, transfer the found measurements to your cardboard, top and bottom, and then simply use your ruler or straightedge to connect the points!

Tricks, Shortcuts, Etcetera...

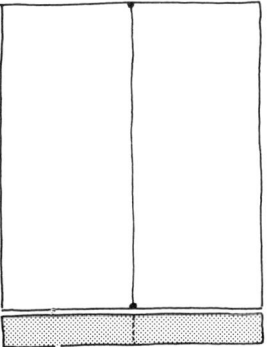

Second Method You have a line that is 5-7/8" long and you want to use your ruler to find the center point. Half of 5-7/8" is . . . ?

1. "Half of 5-7/8"," you moan. "Why couldn't it have been 6"?"

Okay, then, let's use 6".* Place your ruler next to the 5-7/8" line so that length A equals length B, as shown here.

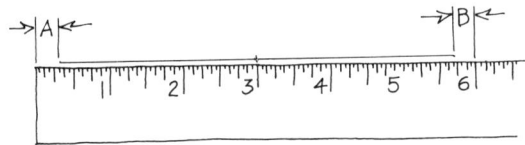

2. Half of 6 is 3, mark it—and your work is done!

PAPER STRAWS

Here are two ways to roll your own. My advice is to use the first (and easiest) method whenever possible and to save the second for those occasions that call for a cylinder of more eloquent proportions!

First Method

Just place your pencil in the position shown and roll, but before you secure the completed straw with paste or tape—be sure to free the pencil! While this last bit of advice may seem self-evident, kids are always doing just that. Hence, consider this word of warning: since a trapped pencil inside a paper tube is as potentially lethal as a loaded bamboo dart gun, I would wholeheartedly warn against using air pressure to solve a problem that can be safely resolved by simply undoing the straw to relieve the tension!

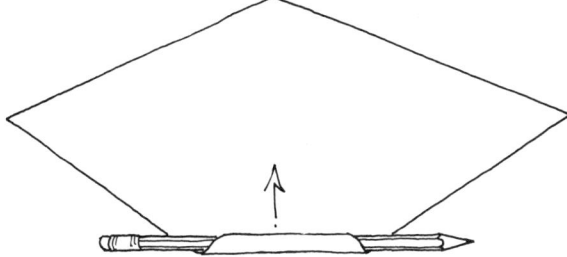

---

* The rule: simply choose the next highest number easily divisible by 2.

Second Method

While this method is more time-demanding than the first, there are times when a narrow straw is needed—and the pencil method just won't solve the problem.

Begin as in the previous method but, since you are working *without* a pencil, do not expect to be rewarded with instant success. Success will come only with practice!

The hardest part is "just to get it started." Then, once started, enough pressure must be kept on the straw so that it will not become undone before it reaches completion. One way to hold this tension, is to push with the fingers on one hand and use the thumb of the opposite hand as a brake.

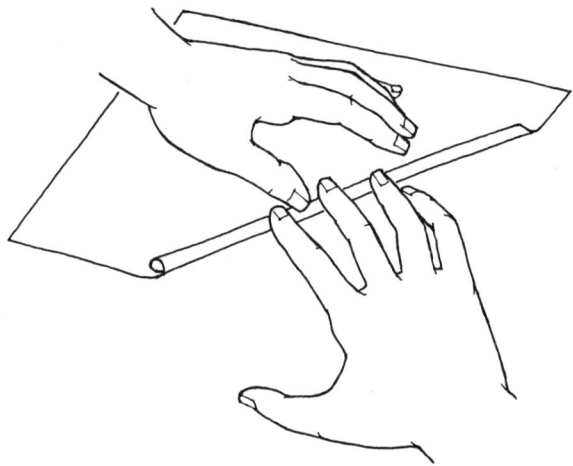

SAILBOATING

Sailboat Fold

One of the most useful of all paper folds is the one pictured here. I call it the Sailboat Fold because it is a term to which kids can relate. (Call it a "Right-Angle Fold" and you'll end up crippling an art project with an ill-timed math lesson!)

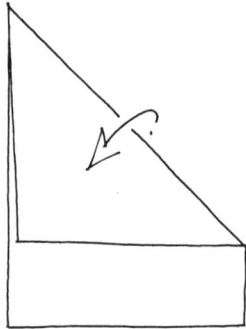

Sailboat Square

To make a perfect square from a rectangular piece of paper, simply "make a Sailboat Fold and cut off the 'boat'." Unfold and—that's that!

Tricks, Shortcuts, Etcetera...

Sailboat Cone

1. Make a sailboat fold, fold up the "boat," and paste the "boat" to the "sail."

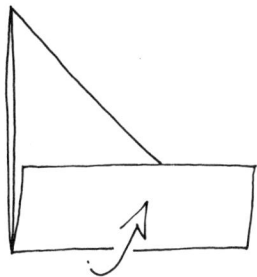

2. Turn this folded and pasted paper over and paste down the remaining flap.

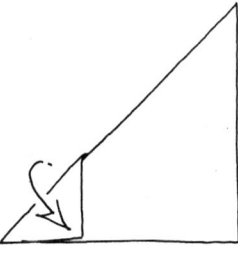

3. And that's it!

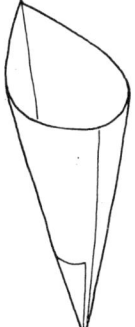

Perfect Sailboat Cone

Use apex A of a regular sailboat cone to swing arc B—C as shown. Cut away the shaded area and open!

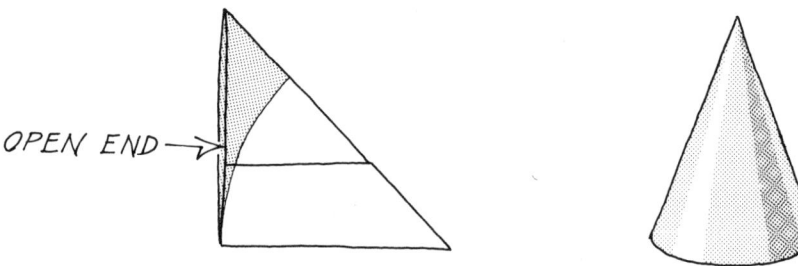

SCORING

To score paper is to compress the fibers along a predetermined route so as to facilitate folding. Scoring is always advised before attempting to fold paperboard and is a prerequisite to all curved folds.

Scoring can be done with a pointed pencil, a scissor blade, a knitting needle or with anything else that will do the job!

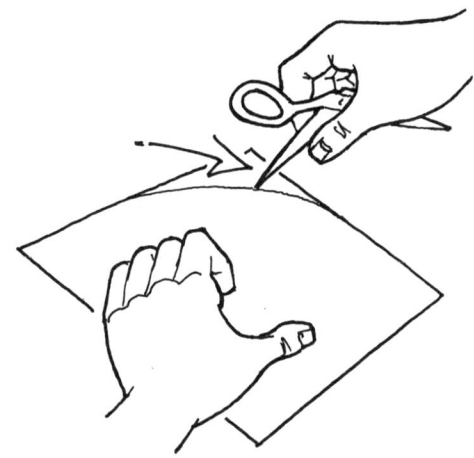

STAPLERS

There was a time—not too many years ago—when I would have recommended a stapler by brand name, but staplers, like many other manufactured goods, are very definitely "not what they used to be." So, when it comes to choosing a stapler, you'll just have to shop around until you find one that works! And if you find a gem among the duds, cherish it—because a good stapler is getting harder and harder to find!

Desk Staplers

While desk staplers come in a variety of shapes and sizes, the traditional classroom workhorse is a versatile tool with a 4"+ throat, a two-way anvil for permanent

Tricks, Shortcuts, Etcetera . . .

or temporary stapling, and is hinged so that it can also be used as a tacker gun. No classroom should be without one!

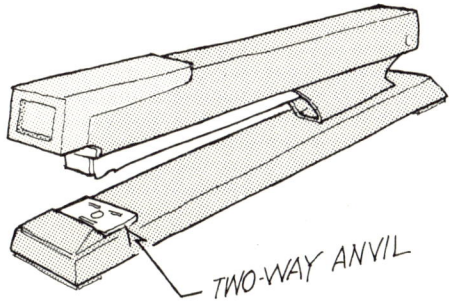
TWO-WAY ANVIL

Stapling Pliers and Hand Grip Staplers

While the large desk stapler can perform a multitude of varied chores, it lacks the portability of the stapling plier. Not only is the stapling plier the perfect tool for ambulatory work, but its narrow lower jaw allows it to plant staples in areas where desk staplers cannot go.

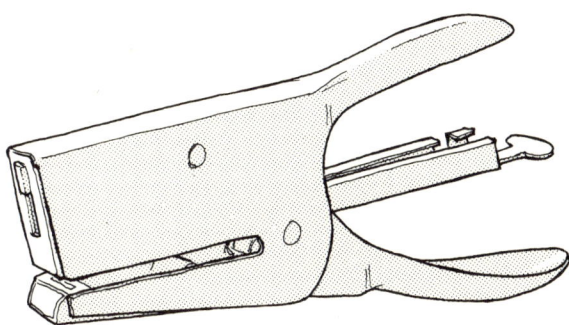

Although the smaller hand-grip stapler not only performs the same function as the stapling plier but tacks as well, for sustained use it is not highly recommended. As a tacker, it lacks the heft of a larger stapler, and—unless you have the physique of a thumb wrestler—it uses muscles that you may not have!

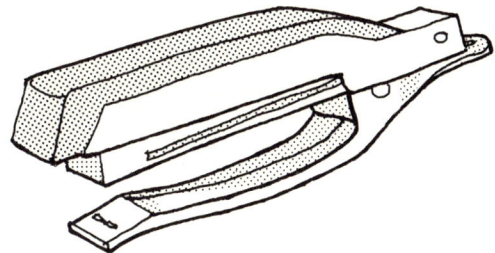

AND FINALLY...

This book can be purchased directly from the publisher. If you would like to order a copy or to inquire about other books in this series, just drop a line to:

Parker Publishing Company, Inc.
Book Distribution Center
Route 59 at Brookhill Drive
West Nyack, NY 10995-9901